Fleeing from the Hunter

D1296969

THE AZRIELI SERIES OF HOLOCAUST SURVIVOR MEMOIRS: PUBLISHED TITLES

ENGLISH TITLES

Album of My Life by Ann Szedlecki
Bits and Pieces by Henia Reinhartz
A Drastic Turn of Destiny by Fred Mann
E/96: Fate Undecided by Paul-Henri Rips
Fleeing from the Hunter by Marian Domanski
From Generation to Generation by Agnes Tomasov
Gatehouse to Hell by Felix Opatowski
Getting Out Alive by Tommy Dick
If Home Is Not Here by Max Bornstein
Knocking on Every Door by Anka Voticky
Little Girl Lost by Betty Rich
Memories from the Abyss by William Tannenzapf / *But I Had a Happy Childhood* by
    Renate Krakauer
The Shadows Behind Me by Willie Sterner
Spring's End by John Freund
Tenuous Threads by Judy Abrams / *One of the Lucky Ones*
    by Eva Felsenburg Marx
Under the Yellow and Red Stars by Alex Levin
The Violin by Rachel Shtibel / *A Child's Testimony* by Adam Shtibel

TITRES FRANÇAIS

L'Album de ma vie par Ann Szedlecki
Cachée par Marguerite Elias Quddus
Étoile jaune, étoile rouge par Alex Levin
La Fin du printemps par John Freund
Fragments de ma vie par Henia Reinhartz
Frapper à toutes les portes par Anka Voticky
De génération en génération par Agnes Tomasov
Matricule E/96 par Paul-Henri Rips
Objectif : survivre par Tommy Dick
Souvenirs de l'abîme par William Tannenzapf / *Le Bonheur de l'innocence* par
    Renate Krakauer
Un terrible revers de fortune par Fred Mann
Traqué par Marian Domanski
Le Violon par Rachel Shtibel / *Témoignage d'un enfant* par Adam Shtibel

Fleeing from the Hunter
Marian Domanski

(FORMERLY MARIAN FINKELMAN)

SECOND PRINTING
Copyright © 2012 The Azrieli Foundation and others

The Azrieli Foundation
www.azrielifoundation.org

Cover and book design by Mark Goldstein
Endpaper maps by Martin Gilbert
Inside maps by François Blanc

LIBRARY AND ARCHIVES CANADA CATALOGUING IN PUBLICATION

Domanski, Marian, 1928–2012
    Fleeing from the hunter/ Marian Domanski.

(The Azrieli series of Holocaust survivor memoirs ; 3)
Includes bibliographical references and index.
ISBN 978-1-897470-17-6

1. Domanski, Marian, 1928–2012. 2. Holocaust, Jewish (1939–1945) – Poland – Personal narratives. 3. Holocaust survivors – Canada – Biography. 4. Polish Canadians--Biography. I. Title. II. Series: Azrieli series of Holocaust survivor memoirs 3

DS134.72.D66A3 2010   940.53'18092   C2010-905720-1

PRINTED IN CANADA

The Azrieli Series of Holocaust Survivor Memoirs

Contents

Series Preface: In their own words. . .

In telling these stories, the writers have liberated themselves. For so many years we did not speak about it, even when we became free people living in a free society. Now, when at last we are writing about what happened to us in this dark period of history, knowing that our stories will be read and live on, it is possible for us to feel truly free. These unique historical documents put a face on what was lost, and allow readers to grasp the enormity of what happened to six million Jews – one story at a time.

David J. Azrieli, C.M., C.Q., M.Arch
Holocaust survivor and founder, The Azrieli Foundation

Since the end of World War II, over 30,000 Jewish Holocaust survivors have immigrated to Canada. Who they are, where they came from, what they experienced and how they built new lives for themselves and their families are important parts of our Canadian heritage. The Azrieli Foundation's Holocaust Survivor Memoirs Program was established to preserve and share the memoirs written by those who survived the twentieth-century Nazi genocide of the Jews of Europe and later made their way to Canada. The program is guided by the conviction that each survivor of the Holocaust has a remarkable story to tell, and that such stories play an important role in education about tolerance and diversity.

Millions of individual stories are lost to us forever. By preserving the stories written by survivors and making them widely available to a broad audience, the Azrieli Series of Holocaust Survivor Memoirs seeks to sustain the memory of all those who perished at the hands of hatred, abetted by indifference and apathy. The personal accounts of those who survived against all odds are as different as the people who wrote them, but all demonstrate the courage, strength, wit and luck that it took to prevail and survive in such terrible adversity. The memoirs are also moving tributes to people – strangers and friends – who risked their lives to help others, and who, through acts of kindness and decency in the darkest of moments, frequently helped the persecuted maintain faith in humanity and courage to endure. These accounts offer inspiration to all, as does the survivors' desire to share their experiences so that new generations can learn from them.

The Holocaust Survivor Memoirs Program collects, archives and publishes these distinctive records and the print editions are available free of charge to libraries, educational institutions and Holocaust-education programs across Canada, and to the general public at Azrieli Foundation educational events. Online editions of the books are available free of charge on our web site, www.azrielifoundation.org.

The Azrieli Foundation would like to express appreciation to the following people for their invaluable efforts in producing this series: Mary Arvanitakis, Josée Bégaud, Florence Buathier, Franklin Carter, Mark Celinscack, Darrel Dickson and Sherry Dodson (Maracle Press), Andrea Geddes Poole, Sir Martin Gilbert, Pascale Goulias-Didiez, Stan Greenspan, Karen Helm, Carson Phillips, Pearl Saban, Jody Spiegel, Erika Tucker, Lise Viens, and Margie Wolfe and Emma Rodgers of Second Story Press.

Introduction

Where can I go?
The whole world is closed...
Where can I go?

This ditty, sung by beggars in the courtyards of the Warsaw ghetto, conveys the essence of the wartime dilemmas faced by Marian Finkelman, who came to be known as Marian Domanski. Like other child survivors of the Holocaust such as acclaimed Israeli writer Aharon Appelfeld, Domanski had for many decades avoided revisiting, either in memory or reality, his own birthplace and traumatized childhood. Nonetheless, the memories of his pre-war and wartime youth, deeply buried and suppressed, were to forcefully resurface in the early 2000s, when he translated the memoir of Canadian-Jewish writer and Yiddish poet Sam (Simcha) Simchovitch, *Stepchild on the Vistula*, into Polish. Simchovitch was born in the same Polish town in central Poland and this encounter with his *heimat* (homeland), brought to life in Simchovitch's memoir, compelled Domanski to share his own wartime biography with the wider public. His memoir, *Fleeing from the Hunter*, not only focuses on the pre-war and wartime period, but also reconstructs the author's post-war experiences in communist Poland of the 1950s and 1960s, depicts his life as an émigré in Denmark and Canada, and reflects on his newly re-established connection to his birthplace.

Domanski was born in Otwock, Poland, a small town twenty-eight kilometres from the capital. Prior to the outbreak of World War II, the town had enjoyed a reputation as an excellent health spa and summer resort that was very popular among Warsaw's Jewish middle class. Authors like Isaac Bashevis Singer, a Jewish writer and Nobel Prize winner, had visited the town in his youth and praised its vibrant energy, natural beauty and multicultural makeup.

Otwock was famous for its elegant wooden villas and the surrounding pine forest. The aroma of pine was considered to be especially beneficial for patients suffering from lung infections and mental illnesses. Thus, the popular saying referring to the town was that "its climate alone is the best medication and cure." Various hospitals and sanatoria had mushroomed there since the last decade of the nineteenth century. By the interwar period, many Jewish health and social welfare societies ran institutions in the town. The Brijus (Health) Anti-Tuberculosis Society maintained its own sanatorium, and the Society for the Care of the Mentally Ill established a psychiatric hospital and sanatorium called Zofijówka, where Adela Tuwim, mother of the famous Polish-Jewish poet Julian Tuwim, was treated. The Germans murdered all the patients of these two health institutions on August 19–20, 1942, during the liquidation of the Otwock ghetto. The town's beneficial qualities as a spa were again to be utilized by the remnants of Polish Jews immediately following the end of the war, however. It was here that the first home for young Jewish survivors in central Poland was established in the early spring of 1945, at 11 Bolesława Prusa Street. Next door, at No. 9 Bolesława Prusa Street, the Ostrówek sanatorium was set up to treat and cure Jewish children, teenagers and young adults suffering from tuberculosis and severe malnutrition. In January 1946, twelve individuals were being treated at Ostrówek, the majority of whom had survived the war in various concentration and death camps. One individual was a refugee from the Soviet Union and two others had survived the war on the "Aryan" side, having been saved by Christian Poles. At the same time, the Swiss Red Cross established the first children's tuberculosis hospital in the town's neighbourhood of Teklin, where both Jewish and Christian Polish children were treated.

In the interwar period, Otwock was not only visited by Warsaw Jewry, but also had its own vibrant socially and culturally diverse Jewish population. Many members of the community were connected both professionally and socially to the capital. In the course of the few years that followed 1918, the year in which Poland regained its independence, Jews constituted more than half of Otwock's population, numbering in 1930, 8,055 out of a total population of 13,296.

Domanski's parents, Brucha and Abram, belonged to Otwock's Jewish middle class and were both working professionals; his father co-owned a shop in Warsaw and his mother was a private tutor. Like many other child survivors, Domanski, who was born in 1929, recollects the pre-war years briefly but with a detectable sense of nostalgia for the lost world of his childhood — the wooden villa at Świderska Street where he lived with his parents; the summer vacations in Świder, a holiday resort located only a few kilometres away from Otwock; fishing excursions to the river Świder; the public elementary Jewish school at 31 Karczewska Street where he studied and where he formed a close friendship with Juda Cytryn; and the encounter with the Zionist youth movement Hashomer Hatzair, all of which constitute vivid vignettes of his pre-war youth. From these fragmentary images, we learn that the young Marian Domanski was steeped in both Jewish and Polish culture, and was brought up with a spirit of pride in his Polish-Jewish heritage. He led a comfortable, secure and stable childhood, which was not seriously affected by the anti-Jewish occurrences orchestrated by right-wing nationalistic local Polish youth in the late 1930s.

In common with other Jewish children, the outbreak of World War II on September 1, 1939, brought an abrupt end to this harmonious, happy and secure phase of his life. A sense of bewilderment, fear and uncertainty began to accompany him and the whole town from the first day of the German invasion of Poland. His confusion and fear was magnified by the news of his father's death while he was defending the capital in the Battle of Warsaw in September 1939, and of his Jewish school being shut down by the Germans.

The move with his mother to the newly established Otwock ghetto in November 1940 put an end to any traces of normal childhood. The ghetto, divided into three sections, was shortly sealed off from the rest of Otwock's non-Jewish population. The Otwock ghetto was one of 1,100 ghettos established by the Germans on the conquered territories. Under the harsh new economic and social conditions, twelve-year-old Domanski had to take upon himself the role of main breadwinner in his much-diminished family. Thanks to what was perceived as his non-Jewish appearance, as well as his wit and fluency in the Polish language, he was easily able to pass himself off as a young Christian Pole and would sneak out of the ghetto to the non-Jewish side on an almost daily basis. On the "Aryan" side, which was strictly forbidden to the Jews by a number of imposed Nazi laws and regulations, Domanski would sell various household goods in exchange for groceries that he would bring back to the ghetto. After a while he became a skillful smuggler, not unlike the little smugglers of the Warsaw ghetto praised in the famous poem, "To the Child Smuggler," by promising young Polish-Jewish poetess Henryka Lazowert, who was murdered in the death camp in Treblinka:

Through walls, through holes, over ruins, through barbed wire still I will
    find a way.
Hungry, thirsty and barefoot I slither through like a snake: by day, at
    night, at dawn.
No matter how hot. No matter how much rain.
You cannot begrudge me my profit. I am risking my little neck.[1]

---

1   Henryka Lazowert, "To the Child Smuggler," cited in Samuel D. Kassow, *Who Will Write Our History? Emanuel Ringelblum, the Warsaw Ghetto, and the Oyneg Shabes Archive* (Bloomington and Indianapolis: Indiana University Press, 2007), 182.

Despite young Marian's successful smuggling activities, he was not immune to the epidemic of typhus that rapidly spread through the Otwock ghetto in May 1941, and through other ghettos across occupied Poland. Though Marian was cured, he had to face the painful and irreplaceable loss of his mother to the same disease; she died while he was being treated in the ghetto's improvised hospital. The sudden death of one or both parents from disease and malnutrition was commonplace in the ghettos by the middle of 1941. Such events marked the beginning of a new phase in the children's lives, characterized by a rapid onset of maturity and a deeply felt sense of loneliness.

Domanski recollects that the family of Juda Cytryn, his pre-war school friend, extended a helping hand to him at the time of mourning for his mother and informally "adopted" him, which was not an atypical wartime practice among Jews in ghettos. However, grief interwoven with a troublesome sense of orphanhood made Domanski yearn for a reunion with relatives who lived in the small town Dubeczno, near the Bug River in eastern Poland. Waves of Nazi violence against the inhabitants of the Otwock ghetto and the increasing daily deaths from disease and starvation were also conducive to his decision to leave Otwock for good. In April 1942, Domanski departed the Otwock ghetto and began a new chapter in his wartime biography, filled with dangerous adventures. Recollections of vicissitudes among non-Jewish Poles and Ukrainians constitute the main part of the memoir, and are perhaps the most poignant and insightful, revealing a multitude of interactions and complex range of experiences with the Polish environment, and illuminating the daily life of a Jewish youngster living under a false identity.

Domanski's account of his life on the "Aryan" side belongs to the history of older Jewish children who played an active role in their own survival. In comparison to the history of Jewish children hiding in monasteries, nunneries and in private Christian homes, the history of children such as Domanski is the least documented and studied. These child fugitives relied on their own abilities to present themselves convincingly as (ethnic) Catholic-Polish children, rather than waiting on potential rescuers. When questioned as to their identity, these youngsters either claimed to be wartime orphans or half-orphans earning a living, or asserted that their parents had been taken to Germany for forced labour or been captured by the Germans. To be accepted by strangers even for a stay of a single night, they were capable of instantly fabricating stories of getting lost on the way to visit their grandparents or other relatives.

These children were the most independent and resourceful in terms of efforts to survive. They were smart and streetwise, having escaped from the ghetto they now used every possible secluded public space as daytime and nighttime shelters. Nevertheless, in spite of possessing sharp wits, they inevitably experienced moments of despair, of not knowing what to do next or where to go, or how to differentiate a friend from a foe. In such moments, an encounter with another Jewish child or group of children suffering from the same predicament invariably lightened the burden of loneliness and brought a momentary happiness, as poignantly expressed in the early post-war testimony of one such child:

It was very difficult for me, and I didn't know where to go, whom I could get advice from, or what to do. I thought to myself that whatever would be, would be. I didn't go in the direction of the town, but toward the fields, and moreover not on the roads but through the fields themselves. It became dark and I went on alone. There was a pile of hay by the road. It was very cold, and I was freezing. I crawled inside the haystack and fell asleep. I slept deeply, and came out as the day began. I finished eating whatever bread I had left, and went on. I entered a young forest, where I met an entire group of Jewish boys and girls from our town of Komarów, all of whom just like myself had been forced to leave behind their [peasant] bosses and wander around in the forest.

This gladdened me a bit and made my heart lighter. I talked with them about my mother and brother, but nobody knew anything. We said amongst ourselves that a cat and a dog were better off than us: a cat has a house, and a dog has a doghouse, but we were chased like hares from one place to another. We stuck together in the meantime – we were eight boys and two girls. All of us were young children. The eldest was seventeen years old, and the youngest was a little girl who was perhaps only eight. We lived very well together, dividing the bread amongst ourselves.[2]

Many of these children had to relocate again and again outside the ghettos. Generally they were obliged to abandon familiar towns for unfamiliar countryside where they worked as farmhands for farmers who either treated them kindly, humanely and with compassion, or exploited them as cheap labour. Some farmers, finding these vulnerable young fugitives to be Jewish, protected them in spite of such "dangerous" knowledge. Other farmers, having discovered their farmhand to be Jewish, would mistreat the child verbally and physically, chase the child away or threaten the child with denunciation to the Germans. Domanski is a sharp observer of human behaviour and his memoir brings to life just such a varied mosaic of experiences – both positive and negative – with Polish and Ukrainian farmers, as well as with Jewish adults, strangers and family.

Domanski carefully delineates the small, mixed populations of Polish and Ukrainian villages such as Kozaki, Barczewo, Persow, Ustrzesz, Sokoły and Ossowa in southeastern Poland, where he worked as a farmhand and herdsman from late spring 1942 until the winter of 1945. During this period he assumed various identities including the identity of a Ukrainian boy and a Polish-Catholic boy named Czesław Pinkowski.

---

2   Yosef Maltshik, Untitled Memoir, "Early Postwar Testimonies of Jewish Children," Archival Collection of Genia Silkes, Box No. 2, Folders 18–35, 15–16.

The author enumerates in detail all the formal and informal attributes of the process of survival amongst non-Jewish Poles and Ukrainians with which he was previously well acquainted in the Otwock ghetto through his smuggling adventures. This constituted an important asset in his life on the "Aryan" side. He was well aware of the physical attributes that characterized both a "bad" look and a "good" look and he knew he was fortunate to possess the latter because of his fair hair and blue eyes. But he was also aware that in order to survive amongst non-Jews a "good" look might not be enough, that one should also be proficient in Polish vernacular and daily Catholic prayers, and to quickly perfect mimicry of all the Catholic and Polish behaviours and standards – social, cultural, habitual and religious. He knew it was important to acquire the formal attributes of Polish identity, namely a Catholic birth certificate, a vital document in order to be legally registered as a temporary resident in any current dwelling. Germans had introduced this requirement precisely to ensure that no Jew would be able to find a home and employment among Christian Poles. Moreover, the young Domanski intuitively sensed that inner assertiveness and boldness were essential attributes in dispersing suspicions that he was Jewish among the Poles and Ukrainians that he encountered. His memoir reveals that emotional attachments and fondness for a Jewish fugitive on the part of the employer might, on occasion, be an important factor, determining the overall treatment of the young employee.

Domanski ceased to be a farmhand in the winter of 1945, a few months after the Red Army entered the southeastern territories of Poland. His subsequent recollections of the early post-war period tell a story common among many child Holocaust survivors. Five thousand Jewish child survivors were registered by the Central Committee of Polish Jews in the summer of 1945, amongst them active child survivors like Domanski, as well as those who emerged from hiding in the homes of individual Catholics, in state orphanages, and in Catholic convents and monasteries. This figure of 5,000 child survivors is not definitive, as it did not include all the young survivors from Nazi-occupied Poland, nor those Polish-Jewish children who, along with their families, had survived the war in the Soviet Union. Nonetheless, it clearly indicates the massive destruction of Jewish children and youth. On the eve of World War II, Polish Jewry was considered a youthful community, in which the population of children aged fifteen years or younger numbered several hundred thousand.

In the immediate aftermath of the war, the child survivors were forced to confront heavy burdens concerning their health, identity, family and future. Older children and youths were acutely aware that their childhoods had been shattered and that they had consequently been transformed into premature adults with little resemblance to children. They also had a profound sense of the loss of years of education and felt starved of knowledge, culture and learning. Some poignantly articulated a sense of irreversible disconnection with their pre-war childhood and family history. They were painfully aware of their predicament as orphans who had suffered irreplaceable losses — the death of their closest and dearest relatives. Some still hoped to find living relatives either in the country or abroad, but such searches did not always result in the long-hoped-for happiness of family reunion. Some of the orphaned children made the decision to depart for children's *kibbutzim* in Palestine/Israel, to begin life anew. However there were also those who experienced internal torments between beginning a new life in the new homeland and an enduring and persistent yearning for their deceased parents and a now-vanished pre-war childhood. Some youngsters like Domanski decided to rebuild their lives in Poland, first in the city of Lodz and then in the region of Lower Silesia, both major post-war centres of Polish-Jewish cultural and social revival. It was the anti-Zionist and anti-Jewish purge of 1968 that forced many of them to leave Poland and search for a new, more welcoming homeland. For Domanski and his family, Denmark was the first stop-over on the way to Canada. Hence he belongs to that particular and vibrant Toronto community of child

Holocaust survivors from Poland whose post-war history deserves a monograph on its own.

Domanski's memoir tells us a moving story of immense courage and resilience. It stands as a testimony to hope and optimism in the face of striving against all odds. Finally and essentially, it reveals how emotionally significant it is for the uprooted child survivor to be physically and spiritually reconnected with his birthplace after long decades of absence. In his memoir, Domanski pays tribute to those Christian-Polish inhabitants of Otwock who today mourn and regularly commemorate the murdered world of Otwock Jews, and to those local Christian Poles, both living and dead, who risked their lives during the war to save a few Otwock Jews. Domanski is one of the few remaining survivors who can remember Otwock as a vibrant pre-war multicultural town and community – a place that is gone forever. His memoir should be of particular interest to those who wish to learn about the fate of Polish-Jewish children during the war, and about the active and heroic role they played in their own survival.

Joanna B. Michlic
Hadassah Brandeis Institute, Brandeis University
2010

SELECTED SOURCES:

Appelfeld, Aharon. *The Story of a Life: A Memoir*. New York: Schocken, 2004.

Bogner, Nachum. *At the Mercy of Strangers: The Rescue of Hidden Jewish Children in Poland*. Jerusalem: Yad Vashem, 2009.

Dobroszycki, Lucjan. "Re-emergence and decline of a community: The numerical size of the Jewish population in Poland, 1944–47." *YIVO Annual* 21 (1993): 3–32.

_____. *Survivors of the Holocaust in Poland: A Portrait Based on Jewish Community Records 1944–1947*. Armonk, NY and London: M. E. Sharpe, 1994.

"Early Postwar Testimonies of Jewish Children," Archival Collection of Genia Silkes, Box No. 2, Folders 18–35.

Friedländer, Saul. *When Memory Comes*. New York: Farrar Straus Giroux, 1979.

Gutenbaum, Jakub and Agnieszka Latala, eds. *The Last Eyewitnesses: Children of the Holocaust Speak*, Vol. 2. Evanston, Illinois: Northwestern University Press, 2005.

Gutman, Israel, Israel Gutman, Sara Bender and Shmuel Krakowski, eds. *The Encyclopedia of the Righteous Among the Nations, Rescuers of Jews during the Holocaust. Poland*. Jerusalem: Yad Vashem, 2004. (Polish translation 2010).

Kassow, Samuel D. *Who Will Write Our History? Emanuel Ringelblum, the Warsaw Ghetto, and the Oyneg Shabes Archive*. Bloomington and Indianapolis: Indiana University Press, 2007.

Michlic, Joanna B. *Jewish Children in Nazi-Occupied Poland: Survival and Polish-Jewish Relations During the Holocaust as Reflected in Early Postwar Recollections*. Search and Research – Lectures and Papers, Jerusalem, Yad Vashem, 2008.

_____. "The raw memory of war: Early postwar testimonies of children in Dom Dziecka in Otwock." *Yad Vashem Studies* 37(1) (2009): 11–52.

_____. "'Who am I?' The identity of Jewish children in Poland, 1945–1949." *Focusing on Memorialization of the Holocaust, Polin* 20 (2007): 98–121.

Patt, Avinoam J. *Finding Home and Homeland: Jewish Youth and Zionism in the Aftermath of the Holocaust*. Detroit: Wayne State University Press, 2009.

Symchowicz, Symcha. *Stepchild on the Vistula*. Toronto: self-published, 1994.

Szymańska, Sylwia. *Ludność Żydowska w Otwocku podczas drugiej wojny światowej*. Warsaw: Żydowski Instytut Historyczny, 2002.

Tec, Nechama. *Dry Tears: The Story of a Lost Childhood*. New York: Oxford University Press, 1984.

_____. *When Light Pierced the Darkness: Christian Rescuers of Jews in Nazi-Occupied Poland*. New York: Oxford: Oxford University Press, 1986.

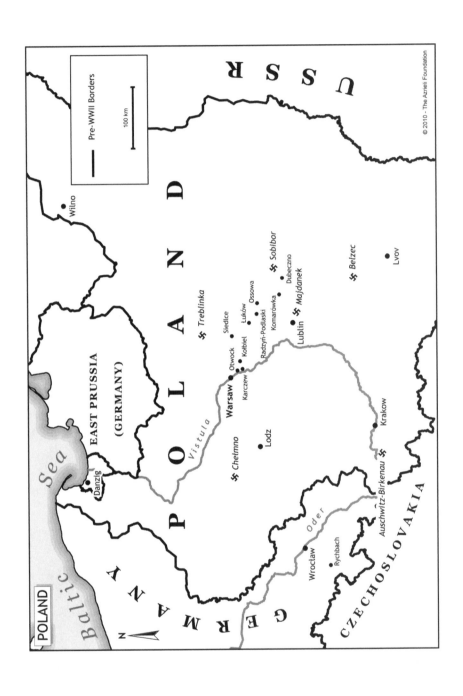

POLAND

Baltic Sea

GERMANY

EAST PRUSSIA (GERMANY)

POLAND

USSR

CZECHOSLOVAKIA

Danzig

Wilno

Vistula

Oder

Chełmno

Łodz

Warsaw
Otwock
Karczew
Kolbiel
Radzyń-Podlaski
Łuków
Ossowa
Komarówka
Siedlce
Treblinka
Dubeczno
Sobibor
Lublin
Majdanek
Belzec
Lvov

Wrocław
Rychbach
Auschwitz-Birkenau
Krakow

Pre-WWII Borders

100 km

N

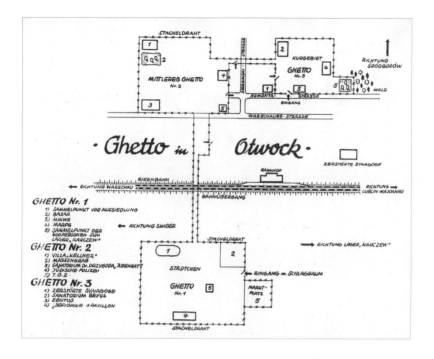

Ghetto No. 1 (*Mittleres*/Middle): (1) Gathering place for Jewish resettlement; (2) Bazaar; (3) Mikvah (ritual bath); (4) Marpe Sanatorium; (5) Gathering place for 400 people to be sent to Camp Karczew

Ghetto No. 2 (*Kurgebiet*/Sanatorium/convalescent): (1) Kellner villa; (2) Mass burial/grave site for murdered Jews; (3) Sanatorium of Dr. Przygoda, a member of the Jewish Council; (4) Jewish Police Station; (5) T.O.Z. health clinic

Ghetto No. 3 (*Städtchen*/Small City): (1) Destroyed synagogue; (2) Bryus (Brijus) Sanatorium; (3) Orphanage; (4) Sofiowka (Zofijówka) Hospital

(Map courtesy of Jewish Historical Institute, Warsaw)

In memory of my mother, Brucha,
and my father, Abram Finkelman

I extol you, O Lord
For You have lifted me up
And not let my enemies rejoice over me
 – Psalm xxx: 1

"There was almost no Jew who could survive until the end of the
German occupation without the help of non-Jews, mainly Poles, but
also Ukrainians and White-Russians."
 – Feliks Tych, *Długi cień Zagłady* (The Long Shadow of the Holocaust)

Author's Preface

I find it difficult to write about myself and, in particular, to call to mind my horrendous experiences as a young boy in German-occupied Poland. In the past, whenever I tried to begin my autobiography, I would first write my date of birth. Then, in one sentence, I would state that my parents had perished during the time of the German occupation of Poland and that from April 1942 until May 1945 I lived in various villages, working for farmers. I avoided mentioning any details of my ordeals during that period. I even attempted to exclude them from my thoughts. But I finally discovered that it's impossible to ignore the traumatic events that are embedded in one's memory.

More than sixty years have passed since I, a thirteen-year-old youngster, began sneaking out of the Otwock ghetto in search of food. Now, after all these years, how can I accurately recreate those unimaginably fearful and dangerous days in that dark period of my life? The thought alone makes me shudder. Nonetheless, I have tried to relive those moments and tell about the general conditions of life in the Otwock ghetto. My hope is to leave a record of my experiences for future generations so that they remember this period of total disregard for human life and the terrible results of hatred and racial discrimination.

Marian Domanski
Toronto, 2007

Author's Acknowledgements

I first wrote the memories of my childhood in Polish and then translated them into English. I acknowledge with deep gratitude the work of my daughter, Beata, and her husband, Wade, in revising the manuscript. I would also like to thank Mrs. Bianka Kraszewski and Mr. Simcha Simchovitch for their assistance in translating some of the documents. In this memoir, I have enclosed several translations of German documents that were obtained from the Archives of the Jewish Historical Institute in Warsaw and from the State Archives from the town of Otwock. These documents illustrate the patterns of Nazi persecution in occupied Poland that I experienced. My sincere appreciation goes to the archivists of those institutions for their help in providing me with copies of the documents for this book.

Photographs in the book were kindly provided by the following: Jan Jagielski, Jewish Historical Institute (Warsaw, Poland), Adam Pulawski, The Sebastian Rakowski Polish Institute of National Memory, Otwock Museum; Jan Tabencki; Piotr Cmiel; and Justyna Gornowicz.

Excerpts from Calel Perechodnik's memoir, *Confession* (2004), are also included in this work. Permission to quote from it was granted by Karta Printing House in Warsaw, Poland. Permission for excerpts from "Twigs of Acacia" (2005) was granted by Midrasz publishing house. The poem "Elegy of Jewish Towns," written by Antoni

Słonimski (1895–1976), a well-known poet who expresses the tragedy of Polish Jewry, was translated from Polish by Simcha Simchovitch.

To protect their families' privacy, the names of all the farmers in this book have been changed.

Otwock

I was born in Otwock, a resort town twenty-eight kilometres south of Warsaw. The town was situated in the middle of a pine forest, on dry sandy soil, and this created a climate that favoured the development of health resorts. In 1893 Dr. Józef Geiser founded the first health resort for Jews suffering from tuberculosis, and many other health resorts were built shortly thereafter. Travelling by train from Warsaw, the railway lines divided Otwock into two parts: on the right side of the tracks was a section with tightly built wooden houses, settled mainly by poor Jews who were in small business or trade, and on the left side of the tracks there were many villas. In some of these villas were hotels of varying sizes called *pensjonaty* in Polish. There were several well-known convalescent spas (in Polish they are referred to as sanatoria) and most of them were located on the "villa" side of the railway tracks, which was the wealthier area at the very end of the town. One health resort, the Sanatorium Marpe, was situated at the end of Świderska Street. There, beside the spa, was a villa owned by Mr. Gelblum, where my parents, Abram and Brucha Finkelman, lived and where I spent my happy childhood years. Gelblum's villa was surrounded by pine trees, which my friends and I used to climb, racing to see who could shinny up the fastest and the highest. Another pastime of mine was fishing in the Świder River with the older boys.

Both my parents worked in Warsaw and commuted there every

day via the newly constructed fast electric train, which took only thirty minutes each way. My father was the co-owner of a small variety store and my mother tutored children who attended public school and needed extra help in certain subjects. We spent our summer vacations in Świder, a resort only a few kilometres from Otwock, where many families from Warsaw used to come during the summer vacation months. Among them were some of my mother's pupils, who would continue to study with her there. During summer vacations in Świder I experienced many happy youthful adventures and my life was extremely joyful. I was an only child (my older brother died soon after I was born, so I don't remember him, nor do I know how he died) and I enjoyed this "privileged" status, especially during those summer months.

In 1935, at the age of seven, I was enrolled in a public elementary school named, simply, School Number Two, on 31 Karczewska Street. Although it was public, the school was Jewish, which was possible in Poland at that time. The school was on the outskirts of Otwock, and on my way there in the morning, walking along Świderska Street, I would pass Bezik Bursztyn's bakery, where every Friday I would bring our *cholent* to be baked in his oven overnight for Sabbath lunch.[1] I vividly remember how proudly I carried home the warm *cholent* pot, with its wonderful aroma, for our Sabbath table. Not far from our school, on the opposite side of Karczewska Street, was School Number One, which only Polish-Catholic children attended. Nearby, at the intersection of Androlliego and Kolejowa Streets, was an ice rink where in the winter we could skate for as long as we wanted for just a few groszy (Polish coins).

At school I befriended a classmate, Juda Cytryn, with whom I

---

1   *Cholent* is a traditional Jewish slow-cooked pot stew usually eaten as the main course at the festive Shabbat lunch on Saturdays, the Jewish Sabbath. For more information, see the glossary.

shared my dreams. Juda was a bit older than me and very brave. Quite often on the way to school the boys from the Catholic school attacked us because we were Jewish, and we had to defend ourselves. When this happened, Juda always fought back and even managed to beat up some of our attackers. Because of these frequent scuffles, the entrance to our school was moved to the back of the building, on Androlliego Street. Many of us were happy about the change because there was an open field beside the new entrance where we could play ball. Aside from his fearlessness, Juda also had a natural talent for drawing. After looking at a person for only a short time, he could quickly draw an exact portrait. Our religion teacher, Mr. Dutlinger, used to call Juda to the blackboard to illustrate biblical stories such as Noah's Ark and Moses and the Ten Commandments.

Mrs. Zajdman, my Grade 1 teacher, taught us Polish songs along with the regular subjects. One song stuck in my mind – it was in memory of the venerated First Marshal Józef Piłsudski, who died in 1935.[2] The chorus of the song was, "It is not true that you are no more." Mrs. Zajdman also used to have us memorize Polish poems for homework. Whenever I studied a poem, my mother paid special attention to my pronunciation, and I had to repeat it many times to satisfy her. She explained that it wasn't enough to simply pronounce words. "You have to feel the words," she said. In our home, my parents spoke mostly Yiddish and occasionally Polish.[3] But during those exercises, while correcting my oral recitations, my mother spoke to me only in Polish.

---

2 Józef Piłsudski, leader of the Second Polish Republic from 1926 to 1935, was largely responsible for achieving Poland's independence in 1918 after more than a century of being partitioned by Russia, Austria and Prussia. During his regime, the situation of ethnic minorities, including Poland's large Jewish population, greatly improved. For more information, see the glossary.

3 Yiddish is a dialect that was spoken by the Jews of Eastern Europe. For more information, see the glossary.

I attended synagogue with my father every Saturday. As we walked there, early in the morning, I would carry my father's prayer-shawl bag, trying to match his footsteps. He taught me to be a faithful Jew and explained the significance of the *tallit* (prayer shawl) as an ancient Jewish religious garment.[4] Father also told me about the history of the Jewish settlement in Otwock. In the latter half of the nineteenth century, a prominent Hasidic scholar and spiritual leader, Reb Symcha Bunem (known as the Wurker *rebbe*), settled in the wooded area outside of Karczew.[5] Many Jews from Warsaw and eastern Poland followed him and soon the Jewish community in Otwock began to grow. The well-to-do Jews opened hotels and kosher restaurants, most notably the resort Hotel Gelbfish, which became a gathering place for Hasidim, mainly from Warsaw. In the 1890s a new synagogue was built on Aleksandra Street (later renamed Kupiecka Street) on a plot donated by a Mr. Blass. In 1927 and 1928, two other grand synagogues were built in the centre of town and used until the outbreak of World War II. By 1939, more than 70 per cent of Otwock's 19,000 residents were Jews.

During these conversations, my father told me about his little hometown, Ryki, which was about forty kilometres from us and where many of his relatives still lived, including his sister Leah with her husband and two children, and his brother Chaim, with his wife and three sons. My father told me he planned to arrange a family gathering at a nice place in the nearby Świder resort, where the relatives could stay with us for several weeks. I really looked forward to meeting my relatives, but unfortunately, the reunion never happened.

On June 20, 1939, I turned eleven years old and my mother sug-

---

4 A *tallit* is a four-cornered ritual garment traditionally worn by adult Jewish men during prayer. For more information, see the glossary.

5 Hasidism is a Jewish spiritual movement that is characterized by the philosophy of mysticism and joyful prayer as being intrinsic to the Jewish faith. For more information, see the glossary.

gested that I invite all my friends to a birthday party. There were some older boys I used to go fishing with, and my mother asked me to invite them too. The party was held in our yard, under the shade of a large pine tree, where we spent all day telling stories, joking and singing. My friend Chaimek sang a lively Hebrew song that his brother, who belonged to the Hashomer Hatzair youth organization, had taught him.[6] Under his influence, Juda and I decided that we wanted to join that youth group the following year, although we doubted they would accept us at our young age, before our bar mitzvahs.[7]

Since it was only a couple of years before my bar mitzvah, my father urged me to devote myself to studying the Torah and preparing the reading of the Torah portion that I would recite at the synagogue. The following summer I would be twelve years old and I had to be aware of my impending responsibilities and learn to behave like an adult. I promised to study diligently and to be ready for my bar mitzvah.

That same summer, at the end of July 1939, my aunt, Rivka Rottenberg – my mother's sister-in-law – came to visit us from Dubeczno. She showed us photographs of her four children – two girls and two boys. This was the first time I had seen photos of my cousins. My father had just recently been drafted into the Polish army and had to report for duty in August, so Aunt Rivka was intending to stay with us for awhile. The sudden outbreak of war on September 1, however, and the roaring engines of the German warplanes bombarding Warsaw, hastened her return home.[8]

---

6 Hashomer Hatzair is a socialist Zionist youth movement that was particularly active in east-central Europe before and immediately after World War II. For more information, see the glossary.

7 A bar mitzvah is the ceremony that celebrates a Jewish boy's coming of age at thirteen under Jewish religious law. For more information, see the glossary.

8 World War II began with the Battle of Warsaw, which included huge aerial bombardments followed by land fighting, beginning on September 8, and the siege of

At the time of the German invasion of Poland I was eleven. My outlook on life up until that time was perceived from the point of view of an ordinary eleven-year-old boy. Conditions and circumstances changed drastically, however, and I quickly had to adjust to the new situation. Fear, hunger and deprivation forced me into adulthood and taught me to manoeuvre through the cruelties of war. No teachings of Jewish moral principles by my father, by our rabbi or by my schoolteacher were relevant under these new conditions; instead, I had to conceal my Jewish heritage in order to survive.

～

The invasion delayed the start of the school year by about three weeks. When the German authorities temporarily permitted the re-opening of the elementary schools in the town of Otwock, I began to attend School Number Two again. The walk to school from our home was a long one, but I didn't mind. Walking to school every morning and busying myself there and at home with my studies gave me a feeling of normalcy and made me temporarily forget the mounting difficulties of life under occupation. This feeling, however, didn't last long.

The German Nazi policies were carefully arranged so that from the very beginning of the occupation, Jews were deprived of their basic human rights. Anti-Jewish laws were put into effect swiftly, and soon we were forbidden to attend public schools.

During the short period of renewed school attendance, however, all of us, teachers and pupils alike, awaited the return of our school principal, who had been drafted into the army at the beginning of the war. Everyone believed that he was alive and would soon return to his post. Somehow, in my mind, I connected the absence of my

---

the city. Warsaw was fully occupied by Germany on September 27, 1939, and all of Western Poland, including Otwock, was under German occupation by October 6, 1939.

father with that of my school principal, and I hoped that both of them would return any day, alive and well. In fact, the principal did return a few weeks later, not to begin work again, but instead to announce the closure of the school.

The students and teachers assembled in the courtyard in front of the school, and the principal announced the sad news. Pale, and with a trembling voice, he read the official decree: "In accordance with the instructions of the German authorities, all schools in the Warsaw district will be closed."[9] He didn't mention the fact that only the schools for Jewish children were to be closed. Of course, in comparison to what happened later on, this was a small event, but it was my first negative experience of the occupation. So now I was unable to go to school and had to stay at home all day with my mother, with nothing to do.

Worse was to come – we soon learned that my father had perished while defending Warsaw during the siege. One day in late fall we received a note with the heading *Ostatnia–Droga* (The Last Road) from the Jewish burial society in Warsaw.[10] The note said to come to the cemetery at an appointed time. Upon arrival, we witnessed the exhumation of the bodies of soldiers from a mass grave. My mother wasn't able to recognize her husband's body as he lay among the bodies of other soldiers who had fallen in the siege of Warsaw, all of them still in military uniform, with blackened and unidentifiable faces. But the dog tags on one of those bodies told us that it was the remains of Abram Finkelman. My mother signed some papers and, with the help

---

9 The school closures were one of several decrees severely restricting Jewish life in occupied Poland that were passed between October and November 1939. In addition, Jewish-owned property was confiscated and many Jewish men were sent to forced labour camps.

10 The Jewish burial society, or *chevra kadisha*, is a voluntary organization set up to help prepare a Jewish person's body for burial according to Jewish ritual and law and protect it from desecration.

of a man from the burial society, I recited the Mourner's Kaddish.[11] My father, dressed in his military uniform, was then lowered into an individual grave. A few attendants began to shovel sand over him, and my silent, stone-faced mother took my hand and led me out of the cemetery. I'm not so sure that I fully understood the consequences of the loss of the head of our small family, having been so young. On the way back to the railway station, a motorcade of German soldiers with machine guns thundered by and we, together with other passersby, hid quickly behind a building until they disappeared.

Tired and heartbroken, we returned to our home in Otwock. There we had to face a new reality – we had no idea how we would now support ourselves. The little store in Warsaw, in which my father had been a partner and where he had invested most of his savings, had been reduced to a heap of ruins during the bombardment.

From then on, the discrimination against Jews intensified from month to month – new anti-Jewish orders appeared constantly. One of the policies signed on November 18, 1939, by the Nazi Governor in charge of our region, Otto Wächter, and enacted on December 1, 1939, required all Jews over the age of twelve to wear white armbands with a Star of David in order to distinguish them from the rest of the Polish population. The armbands both separated the Jews and degraded them. The Nazis also established the Jewish Council of Elders (later called the Judenrat), which was responsible for ensuring that all Jews followed the Nazi orders, with regard to the size and clarity of the armband.[12]

The winter of 1939 passed, as did the first half of 1940, with more orders of persecution against the Jews. At the time, I constantly heard

---

11 The Mourner's Kaddish is a special prayer recited as part of the mourning rituals in Jewish prayer services as well as at funerals and memorials. For more information, see the glossary.

12 Jewish Councils were established by the Nazis to implement their orders. For more information, see Judenrat in the glossary.

people talking about the worsening situation, wondering what might happen to the Jews next. Not long afterward, the Germans answered those questions. In the beginning of November 1940, announcements from the government appeared on the streets about the creation of special Jewish residential areas, also known as ghettos.[13]

These resettlement orders included misleading statements to lull the Jewish population into a false sense of security. For instance, they announced a number of administrative measures, such as a rent freeze, in the resettled Jewish areas. The Germans thus tightened the noose around the Jewish population, while pretending to be good rulers and administrators. In reality, according to the Nazis' plans, the victims themselves were helping in their own destruction. The Germans transferred the task of moving the Jewish population to its designated city section to the Jewish Council, the Judenrat. Of course, when the ghettos were being established, no one could have foreseen the Nazis' murderous plans to eradicate the entire Jewish population.

---

13 Under Nazi rule, Jews were forced to live in cramped conditions in designated areas of towns and cities that were usually enclosed – called ghettos. For more information, see the glossary. Also see the appendix for the announcement outlining the establishment of Jewish Residential Areas in Otwock and for other announcements pertaining to the oppressive laws restricting Jews in the district.

In the Ghetto and Beyond

The Judenrat took control of these new tasks and responsibilities and quickly got down to establishing the ghettos. On November 30, 1940, they notified the mayor of the city, Mr. Gadomski, in writing, that the transfer of the Jewish population to the Jewish living quarters in the city of Otwock was complete.[1]

Because of Otwock's specific layout, its status as a resort town and the large size of its Jewish population, the authorities established three separate Jewish ghettos. The main ghetto was in the old section of the city, beside the bazaar at the beginning of Świderska Street and the marketplace on Karczewska Street. The large bazaar area was divided into Jewish and Polish sections, and a gate was erected beside the bazaar on Karczewska Street and Bazaarowa Street to divide the Jewish section from the Polish, non-Jewish side. There was another designated Jewish area on the other side of the railway tracks, among the villas. On each side of the tracks were wire fences that resembled those on large, animal traps with several openings. The third ghetto was in a separate area of the town where the sanatoria – the health and convalescence homes – were located.

---

1 See the appendix for a translation of the letter the Jewish Council wrote to the mayor of Otwock. See page xxiii for a map of the Otwock ghetto.

On January 13, 1941, a flyer was sent to all the mayors and administrators in Poland ordering them to restrict the free movement of Jews outside the ghettos. Copies were sent to the German military police stations and the Polish police, informing them that they were now responsible for ensuring that the Jews complied with these laws. Very specific instructions outlining the routes that were forbidden to Jews were posted by the mayor of Otwock, along with a warning that punishment would be meted out ruthlessly to any transgressors of these laws.[2] By the middle of January 1941, the three Jewish areas that had been established in November were transformed into closed ghettos, and Jews could only walk on designated pathways between them – special passages that ran from Górna Street in the main residential section over the railway tracks to the villa area, and from there along Reymonta Street to the sanatorium area. A Jew could only walk through the areas wearing the white armband with a blue Star of David, and only in the middle of the road. To walk on the sidewalk was, for Jews, strictly forbidden. Somehow, later on in April 1941, the connection to the Jewish area near the sanatoria from Reymonta Street was closed.

When I lived in the main Otwock ghetto, I was between twelve and thirteen years old. Although not all things were clear to me and my understanding of what was happening was limited, I can still recall many events, particularly the conditions there. Fortunately, there was no overcrowding in the Otwock ghetto. Nonetheless, just being in a closed-off area and cut off from the outside world created difficulties. Otwock used to support itself mainly by catering to summer vacationers from Warsaw and other places; now, the vacation business had, of course, collapsed. The hotels and villas were empty. With the erection of the ghetto fences, the Jews were also cut off from any business dealings with the Polish population. Consequently, most

---

2 See the appendix for the note of January 15, 1941.

Jews were left without a livelihood, and once they spent their savings they had no means to buy food. People had to adjust to poverty, and many became beggars.

As I mentioned, my mother used to tutor children. Under the German occupation, all private tutoring stopped and my mother could no longer earn a living from teaching. It didn't take long to spend what little money we had, and we were soon left with nothing. There was no way to survive other than to sell various household articles. Many others were forced to do the same, so the number of people selling goods multiplied and the prices went down. We struggled to stay alive by selling even our most precious belongings. By accompanying my mother to the bazaar, I gradually learned the prices of clothing and other items we sold, as well as of the essential products we had to buy, and how to examine them and bargain. From the early spring of 1941, I began trading our household articles for food. Then, at some point, I ventured outside the ghetto with a small parcel that an acquaintance of my mother's had asked me to deliver to her friend.

On the day I left the ghetto for the first time it was early in the morning and I took a fairly complicated route through the bazaar. When I had been there with my mother, I had noticed that many of the stalls along the back of the aisles were empty, so I climbed up on the roof of one of them and hopped from roof to roof until I was on the "other side" of the ghetto fence. Once I was on the other side I delivered the parcel to the proper address and wandered around for several hours outside the ghetto, through familiar streets that were now *judenrein* – the Nazi term meaning "free of Jews"– their former Jewish merchants and villa dwellers having been moved to the ghetto. I was clean and well-dressed, without my compulsory armband, and my Polish was impeccable; nobody suspected that I was a boy from the ghetto. This encouraged me to enter a few stores to buy bread and other products. In the afternoon, I returned to the ghetto the same way I had left. This was the beginning of my career as a smuggler.

From what I've learned since, the Otwock ghetto was less crowded than other ghettos in Poland, but malnutrition and the deteriorating sanitary conditions resulted in the outbreak and spreading of illnesses, especially typhus. It began with individual cases, but quickly grew into an epidemic. Eventually, nearly everyone was stricken with it. Many families hid the illness in order not to be sent to quarantine areas.[3] Hunger, like the illness epidemic, also began with individual people and families but soon spread to most of the people in the closed ghetto. One could see starving people with grey-blue faces on the streets, walking on swollen legs in their brave search for food. Food was constantly on every ghetto-dweller's mind. Everyone was talking about food; shortages were increasing every day and people were in danger of dying from starvation. They became desperate and panicky. Hunger, combined with sickness, began to decimate the Jewish population of Otwock.

Death was all around and funerals were a common sight. Carts with the deceased continually moved along Karczewska Street, crossing the gate beside the bazaar. This was a tragic irony – while living Jews were forbidden under threat of death to leave the enclosed ghetto, even for very important reasons, dead Jews were allowed to be carried out to the cemetery that was situated on a sandy dune near the little town of Karczew.

Since there was no means of earning a living, and eventually no demand for home articles in the ghetto, desperation made some people turn to markets outside of the ghetto, which was now referred to as the "Aryan" side of town. Many people had friends on the other side and everyone knew about what was going on. Of course, it was also understood that anyone caught outside the ghetto would be shot or sent to a concentration camp. But in the closed ghetto, people

---

3   At the end of May 1941, the Germans issued a special order regarding typhus in the Jewish Areas of Residence that prohibited Jews from leaving the ghetto under any circumstances. See the appendix.

were dying of hunger and disease anyway, so what threat could the German order not to leave the ghetto hold?

It became a choice of dying from hunger by simply staying put or leaving the ghetto and risking our lives to obtain food. Whoever was able to sneak out of the ghetto to sell possessions and buy some food, did so. Many succeeded, but some were not so fortunate and never returned. The *szmalcowniks* – denouncers – took care of them.[4] Not only were adults involved in these degrading dealings outside the ghetto, but also young boys like me.

After my first successful venture out of the ghetto, I tried to sneak out again beneath the gate that divided the sections, but I was caught and beaten with a rubber bat by the Jewish ghetto police who guarded the crossing.[5] The Jewish ghetto police consisted of about one hundred young male volunteers. Their station was in the villa section, above the rail tracks. Formally under the supervision of the Judenrat, they became a force unto themselves, feared and hated by the Jewish population. This group was easily recognizable, with its uniform of knee-high boots, police caps, armbands, whistles and batons.

I soon found other routes through the bazaar and continued to venture out of the ghetto throughout the spring of 1941. An "Aryan" appearance – I was fair-haired and blue-eyed, like many Polish boys – and a sturdy bag hanging over my shoulder were the main requirements for this job. Also, because I spoke Polish so fluently, I could pose as someone I wasn't, so, with a small package of clothes I would go to the other side and return with food. It may sound strange, but I started to enjoy the thrill of these dangerous ventures. I liked these hazardous excursions to the Aryan side of the city because it became

---

4   *Szmalcownik* comes from the Polish word *szmalec*, meaning "lard," and is a pejorative slang term for the informants and blackmailers who denounced Jews to the Gestapo, usually in exchange for money.

5   A Jewish ghetto police force, or Ordnungsdienst, was established by the Jewish Councils on the orders of the Germans. For more information, see the glossary.

a kind of sport, a distraction from the gloomy reality inside the Jewish area and, most importantly, it provided food for my mother and me.

Because of my mother's diligent tutoring, I was able to speak Polish without any trace of a Jewish accent. The spoken language of European Jews was Yiddish – an old German dialect with Hebrew words added, as well as some words from the languages of the countries where Jews resided. In Poland, except for some intellectuals and assimilated Jews, who spoke mostly Polish, the ordinary Jewish people spoke Yiddish in their everyday life. Because Polish wasn't their first language, many of them spoke it with a Yiddish accent. During the German occupation, a Yiddish accent could be disastrous outside the assigned closed ghetto. Even if someone had an "Aryan" appearance, often their speech gave them away as Jews.

Encouraged by my successful excursions into the non-Jewish sections of town, I began to broaden my smuggling activities by venturing into the Polish villages around Otwock, where it was easier to exchange clothing and other articles for food. In those villages, there were no informants, and I looked no different from any other Polish boy. I embarked on these adventures as an imposter – I had no alternative. I moved around, posing as a Polish Catholic boy, even though I didn't know the village customs or the basics of the Catholic faith. Sometimes I thought of my Catholic friend, Janek, with whom I used to go fishing on the Świder River, but I realized I knew next to nothing about his home and his customs.

Luck was on my side, and the rest I made up with false confidence and lies born more out of ignorance than anything else. I needed to create stories because the women I dealt with in the villages asked many questions. Logical and convincing answers somehow materialized. I used to tell them my half-true story: "Father went to fight the Germans in 1939 and didn't return. My mother has to take care of my two smaller siblings at home." Of course, I didn't have any siblings. But the tale about my father who fell fighting the Germans in 1939 was especially helpful in arousing the sympathy of the peasant women.

I played my role well. Despite my youth, I learned to be a good businessman and I took advantage of the basic premise of a free economy: the law of supply and demand. With a knapsack full of clothing slung over my shoulder, I boldly marched to various villages to exchange my treasures for all kinds of produce and dry goods – grains, flour and beans– which I then put in separate little bags that I carried back in my knapsack. As my business evolved, I learned what kind of clothing and other items were in demand, and if I didn't find them at home, I got them very cheaply from the street sellers in the ghetto.

My friend Juda lived in the villa section of the ghetto at Dłuska Street. In the summer of 1941, when the Jewish police rounded up several hundred young people and sent them away to a labour camp, Juda was among them. He worked all summer long, together with other young men, digging ditches, draining marshes and clearing the ground for a larger camp.[6] Luckily, he returned at the end of November. At that time, some people were still returning from the labour camps. I now assume that this was psychological preparation for the later so-called "resettlement" of the Jewish population – no one would come back then, but based on earlier experiences, people thought it possible.

Juda had a younger brother, Szmulek, and a sister my age named Baila. During the summer, when Juda was away at the work camp, I took Baila and Szmulek with me to the villages several times. On the road, I taught them how to exchange the things they took with them for food. Both of them looked Aryan and their Polish was quite good,

---

6 Marian's friend Juda was part of a larger group of Jewish men and boys called up by the Nazi decree of October 26, 1939, to report for compulsory unpaid labour. Jews were first subjected to tasks such as street cleaning, and then assigned to crews constructing camps like Treblinka and Majdanek that were to become death camps, though they did not know it at the time. The conditions inside the forced labour camps were horrendous – Jews were overworked and underfed, and many were either killed by camp commanders or died from disease, hunger or exhaustion.

and they could have continued in this undertaking. However, to my great disappointment, they gave up these ventures and didn't tell me why. I thus continued wandering alone in the countryside, visiting various villages and living in two entirely different worlds.

~

In June of 1941 I was approaching my thirteenth birthday. According to Jewish religious tradition, I was to have a bar mitzvah ceremony, after which I would accept the obligations of a Jewish adult. This would involve the privilege of being included in a *minyan* (a quorum of ten men), which is required for a prayer service at the synagogue. In normal times, such an event is a happy occasion in the life of a Jewish boy, celebrated with his family and friends. However, when it was my turn for a bar mitzvah, I was living in a closed ghetto and my father was no longer alive to instruct and bless me or to share in my joy. Nevertheless, I wanted to go through with the ceremony, even though it would be conducted in the harsh conditions of the ghetto.

I was called to the Torah in the large synagogue downtown on an ordinary weekday, rather than on Saturday, as was the custom. There was no celebration afterward. It didn't matter to me that it was during the week and without a party. What was important was that I would gain religious acceptance and be able to pray with the other men during prayer sessions and recite the Kaddish, the mourner's prayer, for my father, like any adult. On the day of my bar mitzvah, I recited my Torah passage and chapters from the prophet Zachariah from the *bimah* – the raised platform from which services are performed in a synagogue. The rabbi, in his sermon, spoke of love for one's faith and encouraged me to remain a faithful Jew and to be brave. He also tried to cheer us up by saying that what we were experiencing in the ghetto was a temporary predicament and would soon be over. "The Highest One, blessed be His Holy Name, is testing us Jews in these hard times," the rabbi declared. He told us not to lose hope and that the difficult times would soon pass.

My bar mitzvah allowed me to achieve a spiritual connection and forget, for a short while, the terrible conditions imposed upon us in the ghetto. The preparation for my bar mitzvah had also caused me to interrupt my smuggling activities for some time, and our lack of food had quickly become critical. Parents usually provide the necessities of life for their family, but in my case, in 1941, I had to take care of, and obtain food for, my mother and myself.

After my bar mitzvah, I resumed my smuggling activities. I continued to find good routes, and it wasn't difficult to sneak out of the ghetto. Since I was familiar with every street and corner of the main ghetto as well as of the villa district, I was able to cross over to the other side without any difficulty. These crossings gave me great satisfaction each time I succeeded.

At first, my usual route was to walk along Świderska Street to the outskirts of town through an area called Kresy, where I arrived at the narrow-gauge tracks of the small train – *kolejka* in Polish – that ran from Warsaw up to the town of Karczew. I crossed the open field on the other side of the tracks and walked about four kilometres from Otwock to Karczew. Outside the town there were paths that led to several villages that I began to visit, such as Janów and Brzezinka. Later, I decided to venture into other villages and I walked further through the open fields, across narrow tracks, up to the dike along the banks of the Vistula River. The town of Karczew could be seen on the left of the dike, to the right was a majestic view of the Vistula, and further on one could see the town of Góra Kalwaria on the other bank. To the left of the river and dike were a number of villages in which I began trading, including Glinki and the village of Kepa-nad Odrzańska.

When I wandered to these different villages further from Otwock, I often had to stay overnight. Eventually, by chance, I discovered something that helped me immensely – the proper method of obtaining a night's lodging. A woman I met suggested that I contact the village administrator and a new horizon opened up for me. I learned that to get accommodation "legally" I had to apply to the *soltys*, or village administrator. On a piece of paper he would write down the name of a farmer with whom I could stay overnight and where I would get an evening meal and, in the morning, an ample breakfast – no questions asked.

In order to make my Polish Catholic identity more convincing, I bought a catechism book in order to learn the prayers and basic concepts of Catholicism. In addition, there were certain manners and customs unique to the people of the countryside, and I assimilated them as best I could. I learned the importance of knowing the village social strata and how to operate by their rules in order to be accepted and blend in. I understood, for instance, that when an adult needed to stay overnight, he would have to show identification. However, in my case, the village administrators never asked for it. No one could imagine that this boy, who requested so casually to be allowed to stay overnight in the village, was a runaway Jew. No fugitive from the ghetto would be expected to approach the very head of a village to seek proper and legal sanctuary. Thus, I was able to move around freely in villages outside the ghetto.

Any problems I had were usually upon my return to Otwock, when I had to cross the gentile area of Kresy before entering the ghetto. Polish Catholic boys, some of whom I knew, attacked me more than once. They tried to take away the goods I was carrying. Once, they succeeded in robbing me of all the food, and I was beaten up. Luckily, an older, more reasonable Polish Catholic boy arrived on the scene and reproached the attackers, making them return my goods, which were considered real treasures in the ghetto. I was afraid to tell my mother about my fights with the Polish boys outside the ghetto, and I never told her about my other adventures outside the ghetto either. Yet, even without knowing about these encounters, every time I left she would tell me that this would be my last excursion. In normal times, a thirteen-year-old boy would obey his mother – but these were not normal times. As soon as we consumed the food I brought home, I had to venture out once again into the villages.

After the incident with the Polish Catholic boys, I avoided leaving the ghetto through the Kresy area and took an entirely new road via Reymonta Street. I reached the settlement of Sródborów and, from there, the Lublin highway. Several paths from the highway led to new villages that I began to visit in order to exchange items for food.

I walked on the Lublin highway in the direction of the town of Garwolin and, about sixteen kilometres from Otwock, I came to a small town named Kołbiel, where a number of Jewish families lived. The Jews there were always helpful and friendly, and I became close to one of the families. I was surprised that no ghetto existed in Kołbiel; the Jews there could move freely and therefore didn't suffer such deprivation and poverty as we did in Otwock. Regrettably, no one could foresee that the lack of a ghetto in Kołbiel was no more than a trap for runaways from other places where ghettos existed – the destruction of the Jews of Kołbiel was merely postponed to a later date.[7]

I had a very dangerous experience while venturing in the Kołbiel area. Walking to a certain village, I noticed a path leading over a meadow. Instead of taking the regular road, I turned through the meadow. This path seemed to be much shorter and so I took it, not realizing that it would bring me to a narrow, but quite deep, river that ran right in front of the village. There was a primitive bridge over the river consisting of a wooden log with the handrail missing half way through. As I crossed the narrow bridge, I looked down into the water and, at that moment, slipped into the river. Instinctively, I grabbed at the log of the bridge and began calling for help. A few farmers arrived and helped me crawl out, saying to one another, "He's the second one to get a bath in here." I didn't wait to find out who was the first. I was thoroughly soaked; water was streaming from my clothes and boots. Fortunately, I kept my sack with the merchandise over my arm, so I

---

7 The Kołbiel ghetto was established in September 1941 and most of the Jews of Kołbiel were deported to Treblinka in September 1942.

didn't lose it, although everything inside got wet. In this state, I had to walk some five or six kilometres back to Kołbiel, where my friends provided me with a dry pair of underwear. They then helped me dry my clothes and the things I carried for sale.

~

New decrees forbidding Jews to leave the ghetto appeared every month. Large announcements appeared on the walls, warning of dire consequences for breaking the edicts, and the Jewish police, who had authority in the ghetto, fulfilled the German directives.

In the fall of 1941, the German authorities issued a number of administrative orders that increased the isolation of the ghettos and repeated the death threat, not only for Jews who disobeyed the orders, but also for those who sheltered Jews.[8] I now know that these orders were part of a preparation for transporting Jews to the camps. In spite of these proclamations, visiting villages where life was, in contrast to the ghetto, flowing "normally" and where I could get food, held both an attraction and necessity for me. In spite of the great danger, I continued my excursions to the villages and back. I ventured into the villages to obtain food for our household and enjoyed good meals at the houses of the peasants where I stayed overnight. Notwithstanding her fear and her worries about me, my mother was pleased with the products I brought home. But in the early months of winter the weather was bad, which made it difficult to take my usual trips. The month of December 1941 was frosty and the blowing snow made it impossible for me to leave the town. In the ghetto, people were dying from hunger, sickness and cold.

The typhus epidemic that had begun in May had continued to

---

8   For an example of one of the orders that outlined the punishment of death for not only Jews found outside the ghetto, but also for those who helped shelter Jews, see the appendix.

spread like wildfire in the ghetto and it soon engulfed both me and my mother. I was sick for a lengthy period and, for some time, I was unconscious. When the typhus epidemic became widespread, the synagogue on Kupiecka Street was turned into a place of quarantine for the sick, and I spent two weeks there. When I was finally allowed home, I discovered that my mother had passed away.

Now that so many years have passed, how can I describe how I felt and what was going on in my mind? Is there any possible way to express the feelings of grief and loss I experienced at that time? Naturally, deaths in the ghetto were widespread and common, but in this case it meant the loss of my own mother, the only person dear to me who was left. Bewildered and full of pain and despair, I ran like a ghost through the streets of Otwock, not knowing what to do next. Officially, I still had my house near the Marpe sanitorium in the main ghetto, but in reality, I belonged nowhere. I felt despondent.

After wandering for awhile, I came into the villa section of the ghetto on Dłuska Street where my friend Juda lived. Both Juda and his mother received me warmly and I appreciated greatly the sympathy I found with their family. Seeing how thin I had become after my illness, Juda's mother tried to comfort me in her own way, saying that I would soon return to my former self. And she was right – physically, I improved quickly, but my emotional well-being was far from good. I was completely alone in the Otwock ghetto.

The winter of 1941 was exceptionally bitter and hard to bear. To add to the bitterness of life in the ghetto, the Germans declared that by the end of December 1941, the Jews were to hand over all the fur coats and other fur articles in their possession. For disobeying this order, the penalty was death. In this gloomy environment, I walked around alone, consumed with the loss of my mother. Despite my emotional difficulties and the frigid weather, I managed to resume my excursions to the villages. This probably saved me from becoming psychologically unstable. Outside the ghetto, I was forced to focus all of my attention and energy on fulfilling my dangerous task, and this distraction rescued me from becoming immersed in grief and despair.

Weather permitting, I walked along the Lublin highway to the various villages. I again posed as a Polish Catholic youth, wandering from village to village in the countryside. There was no way I could tell anyone that I was an orphan or confide my feelings of sadness. After my illness, I was pale and thin, but nobody paid attention – quite the opposite. In some villages the farmers even offered me work in the spring to take their cows out to pasture, and promised me solid wages. I tried as much as possible to prolong my stay in the villages, away from the ghetto. I also learned to ask for more than I was offered in exchange for the articles I sold.

Because of the winter weather, I was often forced to remain in the villages for longer periods. When I returned to Otwock, I again felt the pain of being left without anyone close. I felt empty, so I decided to stay at Juda's house, where I found comfort. I handed over the food I brought from the villages to the Cytryns. One day, because fuel such as coal and wood was in short supply in the ghetto, Juda and I began cutting down the pine trees in the villa section for fuel. A Jewish policeman suddenly appeared and interrupted our work. He grabbed our axes and led us to the nearby police station. Inside the station the officer wrote up a report and warned us that our parents would have to be held responsible for what we had done. I didn't mention that I was already an orphan. We didn't pay much attention to their threats; a few days later we cut down another tree, this time without any interference.

At some point, I began to wonder if my dangerous trips from the ghetto to the villages and back made any sense. Moreover, I longed to be with people who would empathize with my situation, relatives who knew those I had lost and could comfort me. After thinking it over, I decided to leave for Dubeczno, a town near Włodawa by the Bug River, where my uncle, aunt and cousins lived. I was only familiar with the town from the map, from earlier correspondence between my parents and my uncle, and from a couple of photographs we had at home. It was on these bits of information that I pinned my hopes that by joining my uncle and his family, I could improve my lot. I also thought that perhaps there was no ghetto in that town – I felt that my survival depended on how far away I could get from the ghetto.

I found out how to get to Dubeczno from the stationmaster in one of the villages I used to visit. A train to Chełm, in the Lublin area, passed by the station in that village and stopped there briefly every day. After getting the information, I quickly decided to put my plan into action. In April 1942, I said goodbye to my dear friends the Cytryns, who had treated me like their own. I knew so many ways of getting in and out of the ghetto that I wasn't about to risk being captured by leaving Otwock from the railway station, or by bringing attention to myself when buying a ticket. Instead, I hiked out of town to the village station where I had gotten the information from the stationmaster, and I boarded the train there.

The journey to Dubeczno, including changing trains in Chełm and stops along the way, took twenty-four hours. The journey seemed endless and I worried because Jews were forbidden to use public transportation – I fully expected the German military police to stop the train and check the passengers' identities. I didn't sleep or, if I did, I could not distinguish my nightmares from my conscious fears. Luckily, no German military police checked the train. I arrived without any problems at the last station before Włodawa. Because the train had changed its schedule and wasn't going any further, I had to continue to my destination on foot. I walked for some time with other passengers until we reached Włodawa. It was nearly evening, and through a heavy mist we could see the city as it slowly became more visible.

By the time I arrived it was dark and I was afraid to walk the streets of Włodawa looking for some of my other relatives, cousins on my mother's side, who lived there. I decided to go directly to my uncle's instead. I asked around for directions to the road leading to

Dubeczno and finally a passerby pointed me in the right direction. Surrounded by darkness, in the middle of nowhere on the outskirts of the city, I felt insecure and tired. I was aware of all the dangers that threatened a Jew at the end of April 1942. I knew that I was on the outskirts of Włodawa, but I wasn't sure exactly where. I decided to look for a night's lodging through the method I had used in my previous wanderings – by getting the assistance of the *soltys*. I must stress that whether the procedure had existed already before the war, or whether the Germans had ordered it, for me it was heaven-sent.

While searching for the *soltys*, I found myself on a road where there were only isolated farmhouses, each far away from one another. These houses were like shacks with thatched roofs. I entered one and bravely asked for directions to the house of the *soltys*, explaining that I needed a note for a night's lodging. The occupants were friendly and seemed glad to have a guest. They laughed at the very official way I was going about trying to get lodging and said the *soltys* lived a long way off. It was already dark, so the farmer invited me to stay the night there. Of course, the family asked me a lot of questions over supper and, even in my exhaustion, I invented answers almost naturally. My reward for telling half-lies was a warm bed and a hot breakfast the next morning. Such hospitality and kindness from strangers! Would they have acted the same way had they known I was Jewish? Or, should I say, would they have dared to act the same way – the Germans were not only shooting Jews caught outside the ghettos but also any Poles who were found assisting them. I had seen posters on the train equating Jews with lice and typhoid, which was supposed to incite hatred and disgust amongst the Poles toward Jews. After breakfast, I thanked my hosts for their hospitality and left for Dubeczno.

I walked for a long time to reach my destination. The little town of Dubeczno looked more like a village, except for a huge industrial chimney that marked the local glass factory. I could smell the smog from the burning of peat in the air and could almost feel it on my cheeks. Everyone knew one another in the town, and I was told where

I could find my uncle, Nachum Rottenberg. His house was located on the very edge of town, close to an irrigation ditch. For some reason, this section of the town was called Argentina. News spread quickly, as it usually does in a small place, that a relative of Nachum's had arrived, and by the time I knocked on my uncle's door, many neighbours had shown up. Among them was a Jewish family from Lublin that had been displaced at the beginning of the occupation; the Nazis had thrown them out of their home in downtown Lublin quite early on in the war. I thought them lucky to be in Dubeczno, where the ravages of war had not yet reached and where the Jews seemed to live in relative calm.

The most important thing was that there was no ghetto in that little town and, therefore, no hunger like in other places. The Jews in Dubeczno were still eating potatoes and vegetables from their own gardens. In Dubeczno, as in Kołbiel near Otwock, the Jews were only forbidden to leave the town, but they weren't confined in a ghetto. And yet, although for the time being they lived in peace, not far from Dubeczno the death camp Sobibor was then being erected.[9] Nevertheless, every male adult was obligated to work in the glass factory for one day a week, without pay of course. Moreover, as in other parts of Poland, here, too, all furs had to be turned over to the Germans and typhus was beginning to reach the town.

This was the situation when I arrived in Dubeczno and met my mother's older brother for the first time. I knew that my arrival would be unexpected, but I was amazed that, for my uncle and his family, it was actually quite an unpleasant surprise. They greeted me with coolness and indifference. I poured my heart out to them and told them

---

9 Sobibor was constructed over the course of March and April of 1942. It was the second killing centre constructed by the Nazis (Chełmno was the first). Gas chambers began operating there in May 1942. In October of that year, Dubeczno's Jews were sent to Sobibor, unaware of what was being planned for them. In total, more than 150,000 people were killed at Sobibor. For more information on Sobibor, see the glossary.

about life in the closed Otwock ghetto, the deaths of my parents, of my survival by sneaking out of the ghetto and exchanging clothes for food by pretending to be a Polish Catholic boy. Although my uncle expressed his sorrow and mourned the loss of his sister, he didn't acknowledge the death of my father at all, and he also didn't seem at all concerned about me. I found myself in Dubeczno without anyone who cared, or anything to do. After awhile, I lapsed into a kind of lethargy.

Where I had expected relief, I found uneasiness. To make matters worse, one of my cousins, Jankiele, who was my age, had a sarcastic sense of humour and poked fun at me. I found this unbearable. I knew that I would have to leave my uncle's house. In Otwock, I had escaped an intolerable situation to find refuge with my uncle; this time, I again decided to leave an unpleasant circumstance. I decided to look for work with a farmer who would hire me to take his cows to pasture. I had been offered such a position before, in the villages near the Lublin highway around Kołbiel. At that time, it was customary for farm owners to employ people as farm help. This practice was so common that in every large village one could find employment. The pay was minimal, but there was plenty of work, because half the country's population were farmers. What I had turned down then seemed to be of immense value now – a chance to earn my own living in a real job.

I wanted to act on this plan as soon as possible, so I began making secret journeys from my uncle's house to the countryside; every day, I ventured to a different village. Once, while inquiring about work, I had a dangerous experience. It happened in an attractive village that looked newly built – in the other villages most of the cottages had thatched roofs. How was I to know that this was a new settlement of German colonists?[10] I was glad to come to such a nice-looking village,

---

10 The Nazis resettled ethnic Germans (*Volksdeutsche*) in some Polish villages as part of Nazi plans to "Germanize" Poland. For more information on *Volksdeutsche*, see the glossary.

and hoped to find work there. Earlier, in my search for food, I always preferred to visit the well-kept houses first. But this time, disappointment awaited me. When I entered one of the cottages, I saw a young officer in a German air force uniform and a woman, the owner of the house. I turned to her, explaining that I was looking for work taking cows to pasture. The woman looked at me attentively and smiled as if she had discovered something. When I began to answer her question about where I came from, she interrupted me and said: "You are from Argentina. Run back to your home and don't come here anymore." She announced bluntly to the officer who was sitting nearby on the bed, "He is a Jew." The officer reached for the pistol that was lying on the table, but the woman asked him to leave me alone. She repeated to me that I should run home. She didn't have to say it again. I ran back to Dubeczno.

A Herdsman's Life

One day I found myself in a village named Kozaki, about eight kilometres from Dubeczno. At the village entrance there stood three crosses: one was Catholic, and the other two were Ukrainian Greek Catholic.[1] Of course, at that time I could not differentiate between the crosses, just as I could not differentiate between the dialect spoken by some Polish farmers and Ukrainian. Ukrainians and White Russians had settled some of the villages around Włodawa and Dubeczno years ago, but I wasn't aware of this then. In some of the villages in the Warsaw area, and in central and eastern Poland generally, the peasants spoke with a special dialect called Mazur. This led me to believe that the way the farmers spoke around Dubeczno was also a local dialect, when in fact it was Ukrainian.

As I was walking through the village a man came out of one of the houses and we began a conversation. I told him I was looking for a job tending cows during the summer. He started asking me a few questions. When he heard I was from a place near Warsaw, he told me that there was another boy from Warsaw in the village who

---

1 Unlike the Catholic cross, which has a long vertical body with arms of shorter length, the Eastern rites followed by many Ukrainians in Poland use a cross with a vertical body that has three sets of arms of varying lengths and angles. For more information on the Ukrainian Greek Catholic Church, see the glossary.

worked for a farmer and he told me where to find him. What was more important, however, was that he offered me work taking his cows to pasture for the whole summer. I had finally found what I was looking for.

The farmer didn't offer me any payment for my services, nor did I ask to be paid, because all I cared about was being able to leave behind my uncle's family, especially my sarcastic cousin. I returned to my uncle and told him that I was leaving because I preferred to be hired in service as a herdsman. Shortly afterward, I reported to the farmer for work, as agreed. So, in early May 1942, I entered a world that was unknown to me, the world of a servant-herdsman in the village of Kozaki.

Kozaki was set among open meadows and young forests where I tended the cows at the beginning of my service. Later, when the grass grew, I would take the cows to the common pasture and meet up with other village boys. I listened attentively to their Ukrainian dialect and soon I began conversing with them in their language. In the beginning, however, as the grass hadn't sprouted yet, I tended the cows on the heath in the young forest. There I met a Soviet soldier who had escaped from a prisoner-of-war camp near Włodawa. The Ukrainians and White Russians in the area helped the escapees with lodging and care. During the winter of 1941–1942 there had been a typhus epidemic in the area, and the master of the house where I worked helped a few of the escaped prisoners who were sick. One of them was the soldier I had met in the bushes where I took the cows. The son of my employer, a soldier in the Polish army, was a prisoner of war in a German camp. My employer would send food packages for the Soviets in the forest hideaway with me as a go-between, saying, "Maybe somebody will also help my son, wherever he is." After some time, the Soviet soldier/escapee disappeared.

My master's attitude toward me was quite friendly at the beginning, and I thought that I would remain with him for a long time. It turned out, however, that it was easier to pretend to be a Polish

Catholic boy while wandering in the villages near Otwock, as I usually only had to stay in farmers' houses overnight. It was entirely different to be in steady service and, above all, with a Ukrainian. This was my first attempt at my new occupation and, consequently, I often didn't behave according to custom. I also didn't possess any identification documents, and when I agreed to the conditions of my employment I made several basic mistakes. The farmer had figured out my identity right away, but he didn't disclose this to me at first.

It wasn't long before I realized my mistakes and why my Jewish identity was discovered; I didn't ask to be paid for my services and I told my master that I had come from the outskirts of Warsaw. Surely I could only be a Jew on the run from the vicinity of embattled Warsaw. The other boy in the village, whom the farmer had mentioned as coming from Warsaw, was also Jewish and had the same idea of seeking refuge in a Christian village where no one would think of finding a Jew. When I had told the farmer that I had been staying with my uncle in Dubeczno, he had known right away that I was Jewish. Perhaps because there was no ghetto in Dubeczno and the peasants could travel freely there, the old farmer wasn't afraid to keep a Jewish youngster on his farm, especially a Jew who didn't look like one. After several weeks, he revealed to me that he had guessed my background from the start.

Of course, the farmer took precautions and told me not to say who I was to anyone else. Stories of how the Germans dealt with the Jews were already circulating among the local population, but at that time he didn't tell me the grisly details of what happened to Jews who were caught. Everything seemed to be going well, at least in the beginning. I trusted my hosts. I even told them about some of my experiences in the Otwock ghetto. They were greatly moved by my stories and treated me well. I hoped to remain at the farm for a long time, and I was adjusting to my new occupation as a herdsman. At the same time, I felt that this was just survival, almost on a primitive level. There was no recreation, and no sense of adventure or accomplishment.

When I began working in Kozaki, I lost contact with my relatives in Dubeczno. Although Kozaki was only eight kilometres away, it was surrounded by bushes and meadows, and I never ventured beyond the village. Consequently, I had no knowledge of the "liquidation" of the ghettos – that is, the rounding up and murdering of all the Jews, or transporting them to be murdered. Beginning in January 1942, this was being carried out by the Germans with the aid of special Ukrainian units in the larger cities.[2] In my childish mind, I thought that if the Jews weren't in a ghetto, things must have been all right. Not only in Dubeczno, but also in Kołbiel, the town I had visited that wasn't far from Otwock, the Jewish population had not seemed to suffer persecution and hunger like they had in Otwock. But this was not the case.

In my ignorance, I had a relatively pleasant time as a herdsman in Kozaki. Once, during lunchtime, after leading the cows back home from pasture, I saw a bicycle in the yard, leaning against the house. It didn't take me long to get on it and start circling the enclosure. I could hear the farmer's wife behind me, shouting, "Look, he can even ride a bike. Surely he'll survive these evil times!" Then she called me over to her and whispered, "Listen, don't tell anyone in the village who you are so that no one can betray you in case the Germans, or the police, arrive. Did you know the Germans are putting Jews into trucks and gassing them with carbon monoxide?" Under her breath she said something about avoiding extermination, but I didn't know what she meant. That was the first time I heard of the Nazis' mass killings, but I didn't clearly grasp the seriousness of what she was saying, as it seemed quite unbelievable.

The next day at the pasture, I met the Jewish boy from Warsaw

---

2 Units from the Ukrainische Hilfspolize (Ukrainian Auxiliary Police) actively collaborated with the Nazis in implementing their plans to persecute and eventually mass murder Jews. For more information, see the glossary.

– Jurek – who also was serving as a herdsman. He had arrived in Kozaki a year earlier. I told him what the farmer's wife had said. He, too, didn't know or understand what carbon monoxide or killing people in trucks meant. Jurek seemed scornful of her and said, "You think no one in the village knows you're a Jew? You see what kinds of stories she's inventing? That's exactly why she is not to be trusted." How could we know whether these stories were fabricated or true? He, too, was working for room and board. Each time the police came to the village, he would run away. His farmer told him that if he got caught, under no circumstances should he tell who was helping him and where he was staying. Once, in the middle of winter, when Jurek heard that a policeman had come to a neighbour's house, he ran into a field without his boots, wearing only his socks. When he returned, his feet were frostbitten and he could scarcely walk, much less run. It struck me as strange that my farmer hadn't told me what I should do in case the Germans or the local police spotted me.

Luckily, during my stay there from May until July 1942, nobody came. Also, none of the inhabitants of the village, neither the Ukrainians nor the Poles, turned us in. It seemed there were no informants in the village, or maybe their hatred of the German occupants prevailed over their anti-Jewish sentiments.

⁓

My life in Kozaki was limited to the short path from the farm to the pasture where I spent all day tending the cows. At night, I slept on the hay in the barn. This, indeed, was why I didn't know what was happening to the Jews in the surrounding towns and villages – I didn't encounter any danger. I liked the company of the other boys and I also started to enjoy my new occupation as a herdsman. I would look after the farmer's cows not only on the pasture where they were grazing with other cows from the village, but sometimes I also took them to different places, particularly to narrow patches in between crops in the fields, or in between crops close to the farm.

One day, I was with the cows close to the farmhouse, on a narrow path between the cornfields where there was plenty of nice, green grass, when one stubborn cow insisted on going into the cornfield. I hit the cow with a whip to get it back onto the grass. Just then the farmer's wife happened to show up to get something from the garden. She started to speak to me in a vulgar manner, saying, "How dare you hit my cow with a whip? I'll put a rope on your neck and deliver you to the Germans!" What was I supposed to do; wasn't I trying to protect her crops? How could I herd the cows without a whip? I had always thought she liked me but, to my surprise, when I returned with the cows at noon she went on about the incident and repeated her threat of delivering me to the Germans. I didn't respond, but her daughter-in-law, Paszka, came to my rescue and said, "Please leave him alone! Let at least one of them remain alive to carry on the race!"

I wasn't sure if my employer would carry out her threat, but her words forced me to decide on a new course of action. She had considered handing me over to the Germans simply for hitting her cow in order to prevent it from damaging the corn, knowing very well what would happen to me. That same afternoon, when the cows were in the pasture, I told Jurek what had happened. He then reminded me about our previous conversation, in which he had warned me not to trust the farmer's wife. Jurek was right, and I made a decision quickly. I told him that I had to go away and look for another place in some other village.

The next morning I led the cows out, this time to the meadow, and I left them there. Then I walked on to the roadway, hoping to find another place to work soon. Having a job as a herdsman was the only way for me to survive. However, I was ignorant of the village custom of hiring someone for the entire summer, before the start of the season. In addition to having their own children tend the cows, farmers often hired the children of poor neighbours. These youngsters spent their whole summers working for their neighbours or farmers in nearby villages. But for me, in the middle of July 1942, my entire existence depended on finding work. I decided to make every effort to hide my identity from my next employer. I thought I was the only one looking for employment, but in 1941 and 1942 many young Jews wandered from village to village, offering their services in exchange for room and board. The peasant farmers knew who they were and for some time took advantage of them and their free labour, just as the farmer in the village of Kozaki had benefited from my situation.

I arrived at a large village and began my search. As it was midsummer, nobody was at home; they were all working in the fields. When I did find people, they didn't require my services. The results were no better in the other villages. I was tired and worried. At night, I found places to sleep in the haystacks, and during the day I walked from village to village, without any success. One day, I hitched a ride on a horse-drawn cart for a fairly good distance. When I told the owner that I was looking for work, he told me that it wouldn't be easy and advised me to go to the village of Barczewo, where I might find employment. As we parted, he showed me the way and then he turned off the road at his field. I continued walking toward the next village.

I don't remember the name of this village, but on the roadside there were farmhouses spaced far apart from one another and I decided to try one. I was fortunate – they did need someone, as their previous hired hand had suddenly left without explanation, leaving the cows in the field. So there I was, three days after leaving Kozaki, employed again as a herdsman, with a roof over my head. But this time I acted wisely and didn't tell them I was from Warsaw. I said I was from Dubeczno, where my mother lived. Also, I requested a fee for my services, and they agreed.

The owners of the farm were a young couple that had recently married. Their uncle, who lived with them, managed the farm and was the one who hired me. During the day I tended the cows in the pasture, and in the evening I helped out by looking after livestock on the farm.

After working for them for about two weeks, the uncle asked if I would agree to stay for a whole year and do various tasks around the farm in the winter. Naturally I agreed, but then he told me that if I were going to be a permanent farm labourer I would have to register with the village administrator. I would have to go home to Dubeczno one weekend, he said, to get my birth certificate, which would be required for registration. It was one thing to say that I was born in Dubeczno and to tell stories about my background; it was quite something else to be able to prove it. To register, I needed a Catholic birth certificate, which of course I didn't have. Thus, I had no choice but to leave and look for work elsewhere.

The next morning, after taking the cows to pasture, I left. I felt concerned that I was losing shelter once again. It was August 1942, and although I wasn't yet aware of this, the Germans were liquidating the ghettos all over the area and deporting the inhabitants to death camps. As for me, I was on the road again, heading for the village of Barczewo, where the farmer who had given me a ride had advised me to go. Again I was wandering toward the unknown. I hoped that I would find a job again with a farmer. While walking, I began thinking about how I could obtain a Catholic birth certificate – I realized that knowledge of the Lord's Prayer and of some of the basics of the Catholic religion would not be enough to help me to survive. I was also thinking about the other boy who had left the cows in the pasture. It was a shame that such nice people had lost two herdsmen in such a short time. Then the thought struck me: the boy who left before me – had the farmer asked him, too, to register and show a birth certificate? That would have been the easiest way to check someone out. If the boy was Jewish, he would have left because he couldn't prove that he was a Catholic. The farmer must have been afraid to shelter a Jew. Once more, I realized that my Polish appearance wasn't enough to ensure my survival.

I soon found myself in Barczewo in front of a house with a sign that said "SOLTYS." Since the administrators in other villages had helped me find accommodation, I decided to ask him if he knew someone who needed a herdsman or a farmhand. It seemed as though he was ready for my question because he handed me a piece of paper with a farmer's name on it and told me how to reach him. When I arrived at the farm, which was nearby, only the farmer's wife was at home, but she very quickly hired me without asking too many questions. I couldn't tell whether she wasn't interested in my answers or whether she was simply discounting whatever I said about myself. It could have been that it wasn't important to her and, probably, she had realized right away who I was because, as had been the case in Kozaki, she didn't offer to pay for my services.

I went to sleep on the hay in the barn and the next morning I began my duties. The cows looked the same as those I had accompanied to pasture on other farms, but here I would be seeing them even more. The farmer's wife told me that in this village it was the custom for herdsmen to stay in the pasture all day long, taking their lunch with them so they would not have to return to the farm until dinnertime. This was acceptable to me. I was happy; I had food and a place to hide from the ongoing dangers of the war. Nothing else was important. I settled easily into village life. At the pasture in Barczewo, like in other places, the boys would get together and tell stories. They were all from about twelve to fourteen years old and spoke in Ukrainian. I felt strangely at ease with them and, since I had picked up the dialect while working in Kozaki, I spoke Ukrainian with them.

It was mid-August, right after the harvest. There was a lot of fresh green grass after the crops had been cut and taken away. During this part of the season, the cows grazed in the fields. One day I was with "my" cows on my employer's field, but because cows know nothing about boundary lines, they wandered over to join another herd that was in the care of a girl and a small boy. After turning the cows back, I moved closer to the children and heard them talking, but the girl immediately changed the topic of conversation as I drew nearer. I had an inkling that we were in the same situation. Several days later, I met her again in the field, and this time she was by herself. I asked her where she came from. She mentioned a small town in the district of Lublin. I took a chance and started speaking Yiddish to her and, sure enough, she understood. She told me that there were eight Jewish boys from different towns working in this village. This wasn't counting the little boy I had seen with her, who, she said, was her brother, but they found it best not to let it be known that they were related. "So far, it's better this way," she said. Then she asked why I had confessed my heritage to her. "I can trust you," I replied. "No!" she said passionately, "You shouldn't even tell me that. I am certain that some day the Nazis will come here and round us up. They'll beat us until we are forced to point out others. It's better not to know."

The way she rebuked me for my carelessness stuck in my mind. She was a little older than I was, and probably more clever. It occurred to me that, since my employer hadn't agreed to any payment for my services, she must have suspected my identity. The circumstances felt similarly dangerous to when I left the farmer in Kozaki and I was afraid the situation could repeat itself here, so I quickly made a decision to leave the farm in Barczewo.

One day that week I got up earlier than usual, left the barn where I had been sleeping and took a shortcut through the fields to once again take my chances elsewhere. I passed through several villages, but no one wanted my services. I had one particularly dangerous encounter. A woman came right out and said, "Now, at this time of the summer? Only Jew-boys are looking for farm jobs." I didn't stay to hear more, and walked quickly back to the road. I knew there was no point in searching any longer for work in that village.

～

What I didn't know at the time was that on August 19, 1942, while I was herding cows in the village of Barczewo, the Otwock ghetto was liquidated. I only found out about this day of horror after the war. With the help of special Ukrainian auxiliary units, the Germans rounded up eight thousand Jews and shipped them by freight train to the death camp in Treblinka.[3] In order to assemble the Jews on the square near the railway cars, the Ukrainians chased the people from their houses on every street. Out of the ghetto population of twelve thousand, eight thousand sat on the ground in the square on an extremely hot day. The remaining four thousand Jews who had managed to hide and avoid transportation were captured during the following weeks, shot and buried in several mass graves in Otwock. Only a tiny number of Jews managed to escape, and even fewer managed to survive until the end of the war. The Jewish community of Otwock was no more.

At times, I thought it was probably better that my parents didn't survive to the time of the ghetto liquidation. At least they didn't have to go through all the suffering the others had to endure.

---

3 The Treblinka death camp was located about eighty kilometres northeast of Warsaw. For more information, see the glossary.

Wandering Again

The liquidation of the ghettos, which had been rumoured among the farmers when I was in the village of Kozaki, turned out to be true, and almost everywhere the news of mass killings now became common knowledge. It was strange, because in the little town I came to next, in spite of all the rumours, the Jews didn't know of the liquidations, or maybe they knew, but didn't want to believe it.

But there was a different atmosphere in the air. While I was looking for work, sometimes the villagers' remarks put me on my guard, and I would realize that they were suspicious of me. I knew I would be in serious danger if they discovered my background. I was afraid to approach the village administrators to seek a proper night's accommodation and also didn't dare ask any of the farmers for food. Fortunately, at that time of summer, the gardens were full of vegetables, so I ate carrots and turnips that I picked from gardens. I slept in haystacks and dressed in a homespun, village-made coat jacket that I had received somewhere during my service. I had cracked heels from walking barefoot, and autumn was approaching.

I continued roaming from village to village, losing my sense of direction and circling among the Ukrainian villages that were located in that part of Poland. I hoped to find a farmer who needed my services – it was the only work I could do to survive – but I would need real luck at that time of the summer to find such an opportunity. In spite of all the difficulties, I stayed in the countryside and explored villages where, by instinct, I felt my survival was possible. I wandered to many places, sometimes returning to a village where I had been before because someone had informed me that a farmer there was looking for a herdsman. During my wanderings, I came upon a village named Sokoły, where a sign indicated the direction to the town of Persow, five kilometres away.

Instead of looking for a job in Sokoły, I decided to go to Persow.

The evening had already set in, and as I passed through the village centre, I walked past a group of women. It was common in those villages for women to gather together in the evenings and exchange information while their husbands talked in another group close by. One of the women asked me where I was going. Feigning confidence, I replied, "To see my uncle in Persow." She shot back, "What's your uncle's name?" She caught me off guard. I blurted out "Pinkowski," a name I had heard elsewhere. She called out to a group of men standing nearby, "Hey, Franiuk, in that Persow town, is there a man by the name of Pinkowski?" "No!" came the answer, but I stubbornly insisted that my uncle did live there. With that, I strode off in the direction of Persow, leaving the interrogators behind. I didn't realize that in that little town, located not more than five kilometres away and no bigger than the village I had just left, people knew each other. And so I went to Persow and headed for my imaginary Uncle Pinkowski, the name I soon came to adopt.

When I arrived in the town of Persow, I was surprised at how small it was. There weren't any sidewalks and the road was just dirt, pressed down by use. On both sides of the dirt road stood single houses with no barns attached. There was only one main road, with one or two shops, and a few more houses were scattered around.

On arrival in a new place it was my habit to explore what kind of people lived there. This time, I was more concerned about a roof over my head and therefore I didn't follow my usual custom, but knocked on a door straight away. It was too good to be true – the people were not only pleasant, but also Jewish. It turned out that nearly the whole town was Jewish and because it was small – similar to Dubeczno – there was no ghetto there. It didn't mean, however, that the Germans had forgotten them. Close by, the Sobibor death camp was already working at full capacity. Perhaps the town was too small for the Germans to be bothered with yet, or perhaps it was their policy to leave Jews alone in certain places, to allay suspicion until their liquidation was about to be completed.

But now I stood before a kindly Jewish tailor who invited me to stay the night at his home. In the course of our conversation, the family learned about my difficulties and my attempts at finding work. The tailor told me not to worry. "I have three children and will welcome you as my fourth," he said. I felt grateful and secure. At last I had found someone who was prepared to take care of me.

As a tailor, my host had customers among the local farmers. After several days, he called me to his workroom and introduced me to a man who wished to hire me to look after his cows for the fall season. At the end of the season, I would come back to my newly-adopted family. To my great surprise, the man sitting in the workroom was Franiuk, from the village of Sokoły, who had said that in Persow there was no family named Pinkowski. So it turned out that, contrary to my intentions, the farmer for whom I was to work knew that I was a Jew. While riding with him in his horse-drawn cart, he instructed me not to tell anyone where he had brought me from or of my heritage. He then made a few suggestions, one of them being that the name Czesiek (short for Czesław) would sound more authentic than Grzegorz (Gregory), the name I had been known by in the village of Barczewo. From then on, I became known as Czesław Pinkowski. It felt strange and ironic to be with a farmer who was aware of my identity. All summer I had been running away from farmers who suspected my heritage, and now I was conspiring with one in the hope that no one else would learn the truth.

The next day, I led Franiuk's cows to the pasture, where I met other boys looking after cows. I introduced myself as Czesław Pinkowski and from that day on I tried to blend in and be part of the community. I was the only non-local among them. Unlike other villages, in Sokoły there were no hired servants except for me; every boy was looking after his own family's cows. But the boys treated me like one of the crowd; they of course didn't know my heritage, and were very friendly toward me. I was part of the group and even dressed like them, with bare feet and tanned skin from being outdoors all the time. I even spoke like them. They were Ukrainian and, since I had spoken Ukrainian before in Kozaki and Barczewo, I had the opportunity to expand my knowledge of the language and become more fluent.

The boys were industrious and I soon learned from them how to weave and shape baskets. We collected materials on our way to the meadows. White willow trees grew by the roadside and by the drainage ditches. At the other end of the village was a forest of mixed trees and among them were slim junipers that were useful for basket-making. I would proudly bring some new baskets to Franiuk from time to time. Time passed and the potato harvest had started and rainy days became more frequent. With a sack over my head for protection against the rain and a whip in my hand, I looked after Franiuk's cows and in exchange I enjoyed a relatively comfortable life with the friendship of Franiuk, his wife and their two children, and the village boys.

One day in the forest, while herding the cows on the other side of the village, I discovered an ideal spot to build a hiding place. Jurek, the boy from Warsaw, and I used to discuss such plans when we were together in Kozaki. But a truly safe hiding place was only a dream. The good times in Sokoły didn't last – the Germans took care of that. In the autumn of 1942, the Nazis proceeded with their plan to eliminate all the remaining Jews in Poland, particularly those still living in small towns surrounded by villages. The time for the liquidation in our area arrived in October and there were soon no more opportunities for Jews to run away before the transports to the death camps began. All of the village administrators received orders from the municipalities to recruit villagers with horse-drawn carts to transport Jews from all the small towns and villages to the railway stations. There, the Jews were to be loaded onto freight trains and transported to killing centres.

Franiuk was the village administrator in Sokoły and one day in October he returned from a session in the municipality and told me I had to leave because he had been ordered to observe the law and register all strangers temporarily residing in the village. As he couldn't register me, I would have to go. My immediate thought was to go back to the tailor in Persow, but a cloud came over Franiuk's face when I mentioned this idea. I felt that he was hiding something from me, and was pretty sure of it when he said, "No! Don't go to Persow. Maybe to your uncle in Dubeczno, but not to the tailor in Persow. It is better," he said. So, I was to go back to my less-than-hospitable uncle, to my sarcastic cousin Jankiele and the rest of that family and tell them about my experiences in the villages during the summer. The next day, when Franiuk gave me some food for the journey, he repeated: "Remember, don't go to Persow!" He knew exactly why.

I left, heavy-hearted, and wandered through fields, meadows and pastures. I arrived at a highway just as a horse-drawn cart, driven by a farmer with four Jews in the back, was approaching. I asked them in Yiddish where they were going. Their answer was astonishing – they said they were representatives of the Jews of Persow and were on their way to Sobibor to persuade the commandant of the camp to postpone moving the Jews to work in Sobibor until the spring of the following year instead of now, in October. Looking back, it was tragic to have seen these elderly Jews with such determination on their faces as they rode toward the death camp of Sobibor to bargain with the commandant, not even realizing where they were going. My guess was that they probably had no one to warn them, so how could they have known? At that time, the exchange of letters between towns with a Jewish population was forbidden. Radios had been confiscated and even the names of the camps were always used in the context of "work camps." Those representatives could not have known what "work at Sobibor" meant. At that point, I didn't realize the implications either. The Nazis were doing everything they could to create the impression that the Jews they were transporting were going to work. But Franiuk must have known something that those Jewish representatives from Persow didn't know, since he had warned me not to go there.

The cart with the Jews from Persow drove on to Sobibor while I went in the opposite direction to Dubeczno. In a very short time I, too, got to know what the Sobibor camp meant. After walking all day, I turned into a meadow to sleep in a haystack. The next day I walked again, and in the evening I arrived at my uncle's front door after an absence of five months. My uncle's family and the neighbours from Lublin were sitting in the kitchen. When my aunt saw me, she greeted me by crying out, "Here you are! Why did you come here? Tomorrow morning we all have to go to Sobibor. Not only that, but we're expected to walk." It wasn't very far from Sobibor to Dubeczno (a little over twenty kilometres), so able-bodied people were expected to walk – under heavy guard. Here the townspeople already knew what it meant to go to Sobibor. The neighbour suggested, "You know what, let's start a fire in the oven and put in all the shoes we have in the house. Then we'll drink vodka and when everybody falls asleep, the carbon monoxide will kill us here. Why do we have to go all the way to Sobibor to be put into an oven?"

I jumped up and shouted, "I will not go to Sobibor! I would rather die from a bullet in my back, running away, than be escorted to the camp. I will hide as long as I can, and if in the end I am caught, at least I will be shot on the spot." After saying these words, complete resignation swept over me and I felt that nothing mattered. Then I said I was tired and I wanted to sleep. I begged my aunt to wake me up at dawn so that I could leave.

I lay down on the bench by the oven and fell asleep right away.

I awoke with a start when I felt a sharp poke in my back. I heard my aunt saying, "Get up! It's already six o'clock in the morning and the Germans might come here to force us to go to Sobibor at any moment." That was the nicest thing she had ever done for me. As I rubbed the sleep from my eyes I saw her whole family, and the Lublin neighbours, sitting stiffly in the same place and in the same manner as I had seen them the evening before. Their faces were weary with despair. It suddenly struck me that cousin Jankiele hadn't said a word and because of that I hadn't even recognized him. I had wished so often before that his tongue would be still, but I hadn't meant it to be like this. From the pile of shoes on the floor, I took a pair that fit me and, without asking permission, put them on and headed for the door.

My uncle, aunt and everyone else suddenly drew themselves up with effort. They accompanied me outside to bless me on my way and to wish me good luck in finding a hiding place. That was the last time I saw them. It was also the beginning of the most dangerous period of my life. It was easy to say I would hide, but how, and where, I didn't know.

I used to read folklore about magical occurrences and, just then, such an event occurred. Was it the gift of the shoes, I wondered? They carried me in the direction from where I had come the day before. I slipped into the irrigation ditch and ran along it to the outskirts of town. A desperate idea had occurred to me – I would return to the village of Sokoły where I had seen a good hiding place in the forest! There were mixed trees there, both deciduous and coniferous, and I would dig a hole, cover it with moss and plant some small trees over it, slender juniper trees. Then I would pad the hole with dry leaves on the inside and I would be safe from the unfair world inside my little den. As I walked, I daydreamed that I had already built my hiding place.

After an entire day of walking, I arrived at the same grass pasture and the same haystack where I had slept before on my way to Dubeczno. The next morning, I continued on to my imaginary destination. Then, having nowhere else to go, I decided to return to Franiuk. I thought he would support my childish idea and permit me to build a hiding place on his land. But this time, when I approached the house where I had been employed only a few days ago, only the dog greeted me. When I opened the door to the entrance hall, I smelled freshly baked bread. As I entered the kitchen, Franiuk's wife gave a start, as if she had just seen a ghost. She made the sign of the cross and cried out, "Oh God! Why did you come here?" I informed her of the German decree and that my uncle and the Jews of Dubeczno were ordered to deliver themselves to the camp at Sobibor. Then I asked where her husband was and I told her I wanted to build a hiding place in the forest. I said I would need an axe and a shovel, to which she only said, "And if you will be spotted, then what?" I promised her I would say I had stolen the axe and shovel somewhere, but she asked, "Where will you get food?" I assured her I would only come in the dark to her back door to pick up food. She ordered me to go behind the barn and wait there until her husband returned.

When Franiuk arrived, I tried to ask him for a shovel and axe, but he gave me no chance to speak. Words tumbled out of his mouth: "Forgive me, I can't take the risk. I have children! Go away! Maybe someone else will help you, but I can't. Go! Not through the village, but this way, behind the barns, so no one will see you." Then he gave me a small, freshly-baked loaf of bread. That evening, behind the barn, it felt like my world had ended. There was nowhere to go. I slipped behind the barns into the fields to the end of the village and then walked toward the meadow where not so long ago I had been tending the cows. The dog that had often accompanied me walked behind me until I reached the pasture. He then turned and trotted back to his master's house, as if he knew I was no longer the herdsman.

In order not to be found in the morning by the boys who would come with their cows, I went to the other side of the meadow and buried myself in a haystack, crying and at the same time trying to console myself with the bread Franiuk had given me. Then I fell asleep. The next day was very cold and rainy. Although no one came to the meadow, it didn't change my situation. I could not stay at the pasture in a haystack and I had no idea what to do or where to go. I was overwhelmed as I pondered my helpless situation. All around was open space, yet I felt surrounded, as if I was in a cage. Would anyone at all help me? Franiuk had tried to comfort me by saying that maybe I would find someone to help me, but if he didn't want to risk his family for my sake, how could I expect people who didn't know me to risk their lives?

I walked to a village on the other side of the meadow. I knocked on a door, talked to some people and found out that outside the village was a highway leading to the town of Komarówka, about twenty kilometres away. Not knowing what else to do, and because it didn't make any difference, I walked toward it. I walked aimlessly in the rain, on the road that the Germans had planned for people like me – a path to the death camp. But I marched through the mud and the pouring rain with what must have been faith, still under the illusion that somehow, in another small town, it would be different. With that kind of desperate optimism, I arrived in Komarówka.

For a brief moment I had hope because I saw people walking about openly, talking in an animated manner. Then I noticed that many of the houses had their doors flung open. They were empty and people's belongings were strewn over the streets. I asked a boy, about my age, the meaning of all the chaos. He told me that the previous day many people from the town had been sent to the camp, and tomorrow would be the same. Some people were running away to the forest. When he found out that I had spent the summer working as a herdsman, he was surprised and asked why I would leave the village and go to Komarówka. What could I tell him? It was precisely because I had been roaming around in the villages during the summer that I had no idea what was happening in places like Dubeczno and here.

I was tired, cold and wet from the rain, and evening was setting in.

I began looking for a place to sleep. I walked into several homes and tried to find accommodation. In that tragic moment, the very people who knew they would be transported out of town to a death camp treated me harshly. I was appalled. They denied me a place to sleep, even though it wouldn't have made any difference to their situation. Bitterness had completely hardened these people. There was one carpenter, for example, who had a workshop with a floor covered with wooden shavings – it was big enough for at least ten people to sleep comfortably. Yet, he refused me shelter. The carpenter's son, a boy about my age, seemed to take special satisfaction in telling me, "Here we work for the Germans – the Waffen SS and SD – so we don't have a place for anyone to sleep."[1] I left the house and, with dread, wandered toward the empty houses that I had seen earlier. I wondered about sleeping in one of them. While exploring the possibility, I found a camera that had been left on the ground and put it in my pocket. Eventually, I found a spot to sleep.

I must have been noticed, however, for a Jewish policeman suddenly came in and ordered me to go with him. He escorted me to a barn right across the street from the carpenter's workshop, where I joined other people. Then more people joined us. The Jewish policemen were in charge of bringing in individuals who may have tried to evade the German orders. After awhile, they brought in the rabbi of the town with some of his followers who had tried to run away. I pitied them for having been caught. Soon their prayers were drowned out by the curses of newcomers, which were directed at the police. One man was beside himself, swearing and yelling, "Why did you stop me and drag me here when I was already out of town? I promise

---

1 SS is the abbreviation for Schutzstaffel, meaning Defense Force, which dealt with policing and the enforcement of Nazi racial policies in Germany and the Nazi-occupied countries. SD stands for Sicherheitsdienst and was the security and intelligence service of the SS. For more information see the glossary.

you'll be the first to be killed when the transport arrives at the camp. This is the way the Nazis get their work done." More people arrived and were forced into the barn. By dawn, it was so jammed that none of us could sit on the floor; we had to stand side by side.

After that terrible night, the gates of the barn were thrown open, revealing a beautiful, sunny morning. But when my eyes grew accustomed to the light, I saw a long line of horse-drawn carts, one after another, rolling up to the front of the barn. This was our transport. The policemen directed traffic, ordering us to get in and sit down, four people to a cart. It struck me as a rather comfortable arrangement after being herded together in the barn, but maybe the local farmers were being considerate of their horses and didn't want to tire them out on such a long journey. How ironic, I thought to myself. This was what Franiuk must have wanted me to avoid when he kept persuading me not to go to the tailor in Persow, and here it was happening to me in Komarówka.

Waiting in line to climb into the cart, I noticed a narrow gate on the other side of the street, by the fence near the carpenter's house. People from the town were being ushered into the carts one at a time. They had small bundles for their journey. With shock I recognized the carpenter's son, who had been so proud of working for the SS and the SD and whose parents had refused me accommodation. He, too, had his little bundle and was now climbing into the cart. The Germans rounded up all of them. I remembered what the girl who was herding the cows in Barczewo had told me – that she and all the Jewish boys would be rounded up and taken away. I wondered whether she and her little brother had been captured, too.

There was no time to think anymore, however, for the policemen commanding the traffic were continuously yelling orders as they filled the carts in a smooth, efficient manner. I knew we were headed for a death camp. The people in the barn had been talking about it all night. All the rumours became very real. The cart was like a scaffold. I asked myself, "Am I a criminal, doomed for execution?" I was determined to run away and the thought never left my mind. From my vantage point, I could see the long line of carts, filled with people, and the "caravan" started moving. The Jewish policemen were making sure that everything was in order with the carts on the road and the German soldiers, holding their rifles at the ready, were guarding us so that no one could run away. In spite of that, all through the drive I kept looking for a possibility to jump off the cart.

We were driven through fields and small forests where it was impossible to make a getaway. After several hours, we passed through a dense forest, which seemed to provide me with the best opportunity. As I tried to decide which side to jump from, I noticed a soldier waiting behind a tree with a gun, ready to fire. Then I detected more soldiers in the distance, waiting in ambush to shoot any escapees. I heard no rifle shots so I knew that not one of these people had attempted to run for it, and here I was considering it. Was I insane? The horse-drawn carts drove all day without stopping, through more small forests and fields, without incident.

It was close to evening when a young man of about eighteen approached our cart to ask, "Have you seen my parents?" Instead of answering, the young girl sitting beside me exclaimed, "You are on this transport, too? How is that possible?" It turned out that he had already been transported two days earlier. He explained that he had come from the town of Międzyrzec, which wasn't far away. He had run away as soon as the Germans started loading the people onto the freight train. He said that at that moment there was a lot of commotion and disarray. He had been waiting in the bushes all day for our transport in search of his parents, hoping that he could help them escape. He advised us, "If any one of you intends to run away, this is the only chance – on this road, before you reach the town of Międzyrzec. Because once they take you to that town, it'll be too late! Directly from these horse-drawn carts, the Nazis will take you behind barbed wire to wait for the freight trains. Once you are taken into the cattle cars, that will be the end. You'll be sent to the death camp, so run away!" Then he went on, cart after cart, looking for his parents, and I could hear his voice gradually fading away saying, "Have you seen my parents? Run away!" I envied his hope to be reunited with his parents.

Escape from the Transport

Reality is stranger than fiction. Sitting on the cart with me were two sisters and a rabbi. At intervals, the policemen would allow people from other carts that were close by to come and talk to the rabbi and seek solace. While riding in the cart, I overheard an unusual conversation. One of the sisters asked, "Rabbi, does the other world exist?" The rabbi answered, "Yes, it exists." The girl said, "Good. In that case we will be living in that other world," to which the Rabbi replied, "You see, my child, the other world is quite different; it certainly exists, but it's better to live in this world." I wondered what was going on in the minds of all these people who knew they were going to be annihilated; some of them must have had the same thought as I did – to escape.

The elder sister started to think out loud. "It would be better to run away," she declared. She asked the farmer driving the cart for help. She and her sister would jump down from the cart, she said, and hide in the bushes. They would wait there for him to return and then they would reward him with all kinds of expensive goods that they had hidden away. She started to specify what she would give him for his help. He didn't answer. The girl may not have known that the Nazis had issued strict orders to kill those who were caught helping Jews, but the driver must have known the consequences all too well. After awhile, the girl started to think aloud again: "It would be good to have a Catholic birth certificate because then one could go voluntarily to Germany to work there, and it would be much easier to survive the war. Several people have already done this." She began to recite a list of names. Then, again, she asked the driver for help: "Couldn't you help me to obtain two Catholic birth certificates from some village girls?" The farmer remained silent.

The horse-drawn carts, escorted by the German soldiers and the Jewish policemen, were moving without complications and finally we entered a big village, the name of which I can't remember. In the middle was a pond, where the Germans permitted the farmers to water and feed their horses. The horses surrounded the pond. To our surprise, the Germans allowed the people to climb down from the carts and help themselves to water from nearby wells. I jumped off the cart and went to a house located on the opposite side of the road. No one was following me. Although some people, like me, were running in different directions to find water, others didn't leave and simply sat in the carts, barely moving. As I approached the well, I didn't see anyone on the farm. It was the potato harvest and it was possible that they hadn't yet returned from the field. I passed the well without stopping to drink and went in the direction of the barn. From there, a footpath led to a little gate in the fence that enclosed a garden, and then continued to a meadow where I could see a haystack. I walked ahead, not daring to look back. I felt terribly anxious. Perhaps a German soldier in ambush would shoot me. Or maybe someone would find me and force me back to the transport. It was better not to look back.

Only when I was safely behind the haystack did I venture to look around. I didn't see anyone. I was standing and listening, my heart pounding. It was hard to believe that I was free again. It was a beautiful autumn day, the sun was setting, and for me everything was beautiful again. I pulled hay from the haystack to make a hole, and while I buried myself inside, I heard noises from the village – yelling and rifle shots. The tumult could not have lasted long, but to me it seemed like ages. I was sure that someone had been shot for doing what I had done – running away. I was afraid someone would show up at the haystack where I was hiding and take me back to the transport, but my luck held.

Sitting in that haystack, I recalled the experiences of the last few days. I thought of how terrified my relatives must have felt while they were transported from Dubeczno to Sobibor. And I wondered if what I had said several days ago in Dubeczno – that I would rather end my life running away with a bullet in my back than be escorted to the death camp – would actually happen. Most of all, I wondered if there was any place where Jews would be permitted to stay alive.

Early the next morning, when I emerged from my hiding place, I picked the hay off my clothing and proceeded through the pasture in the direction of the village located on the other side of the meadow. When I got closer I took a shortcut through some bushes and, at first not realizing it, I found myself in an orchard on a farmer's property. There was a group of people there, eating breakfast outdoors and sitting at tables laden with food. I could smell each type of delicious food, and my stomach ached from hunger. I hadn't tasted a thing except fear for two days. Impulsively, I stopped in my tracks and looked at the villagers. I didn't say a word but a woman in the group saw me and said, "Look, I am sure this must be a Jew. Yesterday they were transporting them through the village." Another villager asked me if I was a Jew. I flatly denied it. I told him I had also seen the Germans transporting "them" while I was getting potatoes. The farmer asked, "Are you walking through villages begging for potatoes?" "Yes," I answered. "I already have several sacks of potatoes in different villages. I left a sack at the house where I was sleeping last night and intend to pick up a little more and take everything home by a horse-drawn cart, if I find the opportunity. Right now I need a sack because I've already used all that I have." He asked me where I was from. I said I was from Dubeczno. I didn't know how far this place was from Dubeczno. From their dialect, I could tell that this village was Polish, not Ukrainian.

Although I had no idea if it made any sense to turn myself into a beggar, at that very critical moment it seemed the only possibility of getting out of a difficult situation. During the German occupation of Poland, it wasn't unusual for beggars to be wandering through villages, asking for potatoes, so my story had some credibility. Nonetheless, the villager continued with his questions. He told me to make the sign of the cross and then to say the Lord's Prayer. I recited it perfectly. Suddenly, he became friendly and asked if I wanted to eat, inviting me to join them at the table. I saw excellent food and wonderful baked goods in front of me, which only made my stomach ache more, but I couldn't let him know that I was hungry, so I controlled myself and told them that I had already eaten a good breakfast. I said I had eaten early in the morning because the farmer had to drive to his field to dig potatoes. He said to me, "We are also going to dig potatoes. Maybe you can come with us to help and I will pay you with a big basketful." I refused politely and, not waiting for another question, walked away.

Instead of going into the village and begging for potatoes, as I had just told them, I went in the direction of the train tracks that I saw in the distance. Going through the fields toward the railway tracks, I picked up a turnip. After two days of fasting, it tasted as good as the sweetest of apples. After I had eaten I was able to think more clearly. Yes, I had managed to run away from the transport and I was free, but where would I go? What next? Should I ask someone to help me hide, as Franiuk had suggested? I didn't want to take the chance of putting others at risk, since the Nazis had warned the Polish and Ukrainian populace that anyone assisting Jews by any means would be subject to the death penalty. Under these circumstances, what chance would a Jewish boy who had just run away from a transport have? Where could I expect any help?

I came to the firm conclusion that in order to survive I had to rely solely on myself. I had nothing to go on but my appearance, my wits, my ability to speak Polish without an accent and, of course, my limited knowledge of the Catholic faith. In some ways, my situation could be compared to that of a rabbit fleeing from a hunter. For a moment the rabbit is able to elude the hunter, but somewhere a trap has been set, ready and waiting for him. I felt that I didn't have much chance to survive. Completely wrapped up in my thoughts, I approached the tracks and, without knowing where I was going, somehow turned in a direction that took me to a small railway station. From the information posted on a wall, I discovered that those tracks led to a town named Łuków and then on to a town called Siedlce.[1]

What forces guide a person's life? Is it God, fate or plain chance? Had I continued walking in the direction of Łuków without stopping, I would have fallen into a trap like the one in Komarówka. But I didn't go there. On the left side of the tracks there were bushes, then a grass pasture, and in the horizon I saw a village. I stepped off the tracks and hid in the bushes for awhile. From there, I could see that it was a beautiful day – I was as free as the birds perched on top of the bushes in which I was hiding.

I was hungry and wondered where I would get food. I thought that the procedure of getting a note from the *soltys* to receive a night's lodging would probably be the same here as in the villages near Warsaw, and I thought that I could take that chance. I waited until sunset and then took a shortcut through the pasture to the village to look for the *soltys*. When I encountered him what he saw was a country boy with blue eyes and blond hair. He gave me the usual note with a farmer's name on it.

For me, at fourteen, there was no problem at all, but had I been a couple of years older I would have had to show some identification. I went to the given address for a night's sleep. As expected, I

---

1   Łuków, a city in eastern Poland, was the site of a large ghetto of more than 12,000 Jews by 1942, and in October of that year, many were deported to the death camp in Treblinka. Siedlce is a small town north of Lublin and east of Warsaw; more than 10,000 Jews were deported to Treblinka from there.

was given a good supper and a good breakfast in the morning. I then went back to the railway tracks in the morning and started walking. As I walked, I nursed a daydream about how good it would be if in the next town the Nazis didn't round up the Jews and transport them to death camps.

Łuków was far away. Why hurry, I thought to myself, when every evening and morning I could have good food? When I spotted another village, far in the distance, I left the railway tracks and, as I had done the day before, sat down in some bushes, waiting for evening to arrive. Again, I had success. I got a note and went for a night's accommodation and food, as before. And so, by day I would stay in the bushes, and in the evening I would go to the *soltys* for my letter. One might say that I even made a good living following those railway tracks. In other words, I temporarily exploited the occasion, without any knowledge of what the next day would bring.

One time, while spending the night at a farmer's place, I "borrowed" a prayer book to replace the one I had left behind somewhere a long time beforehand. I suspected it would benefit me while staying in the villages. The following day I was back on the tracks in the direction of Łuków, contemplating how many villages I would encounter before arriving at my destination, Siedlce. On the tracks, I passed a railway booth the size of a telephone stall where there was a worker on duty looking after junction signals. When I approached the booth, the employee, who had just come back from checking the signals, spotted me and called out, "Hey, boy, why are you walking on the tracks? Do you want to pay a fine? Where do you think you're going?"

I concocted a story in a hurry, telling him that my mother had ordered me to go to the town of Łuków to see how my uncle was doing because we hadn't heard from him for quite some time. "When I arrive at his house," I said, "I am to reply to my mother." He said, "Okay, and what does your father do for a living?" I responded, truthfully, "I don't have a father. He went into the army in 1939 to fight the Germans and didn't return."

"Let's say you can't find your uncle – what will happen then?"

"Then I'll go home to Dubeczno, to my mother, or I'll look for some place to become a servant, because during the summer I intend to herd cows anyway."

He seemed to like my answer because he replied, "In that case, why don't you come to my house? You would be of help on my farm." When he told me that, I had to control my emotions, in order not to show how happy I was. I tried to appear nonchalant and said, "Fine, if I can't find my uncle, I'll come work for you. But if I don't like the conditions, I will be free to leave at any time."

He wrote down his surname on a piece of paper, as well as the name of his village and directions to his farm. I took the paper from him – it felt like a ticket to my salvation.

A New Identity

Thinking in religious terms, one could say that God had sent this man to me. Now, since I had said I was going to my uncle, I had to go to the town to find out what it was like, in case it came up in future conversations. I was curious as well. Thus, without leaving the tracks, I went on to Łuków with a job offer on a farm for the coming winter. I put the piece of paper from the railway man safely in my pocket. On the right side of the tracks was the village, comprised of single houses surrounded by land, just like he had told me. One of those houses belonged to him. Closer to town, and almost by the tracks, was a small house belonging to another railway worker. Close to that house, on the slope, I saw a group of boys watching their cows, enjoying the last warm days of October.

The Łuków station was on the right side of the tracks and I turned toward the town on the left. When I arrived there, I noticed that the main streets were empty, as were some small streets. There seemed to be no one around. I turned back and walked toward the station. By the road, I came across a little store and I went in to look around. Inside, I discovered that one could buy or sell anything there and I realized that I had something to sell – the camera I had picked up in that terrible town, Komarówka, where I was put on the transport. The owner started to haggle, saying, "How much do you want?" "Forty-five złoty," I told him. "Ho! For that amount of money, I could buy a good chicken. I will give you twenty złoty."[1] Finally, the camera changed hands for twenty-five złoty.

I left the kiosk and walked again along the tracks, back toward the village where I had a job. I had to pass some time before arriving there, since I was supposed to be looking for my imaginary uncle. I sat down by myself on the slope, not far from the group of boys I had seen. Five of the boys lost no time coming over to me and started drilling me with questions. Who was I? I told them I was going into service with the railway man and that by the evening he expected me to turn up for work. I showed them the note with the railway worker's name.

My explanation apparently didn't sound authentic enough. One of them said that a few days earlier the liquidation of the Łuków ghetto had taken place and that there were still some people on the run. "Are you by chance a Jew?" they asked. Of course, I denied it. I reminded them that just a while ago I had passed them on these tracks on my way to Łuków, and they must have seen me, because I had seen them. "Okay, in that case recite the Lord's Prayer!" they demanded. This was a repeat performance and I started right in, but halfway through the prayer, the most aggressive lad told me to say the prayer to the Virgin Mary instead. When I finished that prayer they decided that, obviously, I wasn't a Jew after all. They all sat down beside me and started to chat in a friendly way.

After talking to the boys for some time, I went over to the railway man's house, but only his wife was at home. I introduced myself and told her of my conversation with her husband. I also told her that he had been right, because I could not find my uncle in Łuków. My imagination had no limits. In fact, I said, I found out from my uncle's neighbours that the Gestapo was after him, so they suspected he had

---

1   The złoty is the main currency of Poland.

gone over to the partisans.[2] Although the story of an uncle I could not find in the town of Łuków was fabricated, I knew it could have very well been true because at that time, to avoid arrest, many people were running away and joining the resistance. I showed her the note from her husband. Here I was, willing to accept his offer of room and board, with very little pay, in exchange for work on the farm through the winter. In the evening, when her husband returned home, he and his wife accepted my service.

They had a five-hectare farm, one horse and one cow, and I was told to run the cow to the pasture in the morning. The next day I took the cow to the slope by the railway tracks together with the boys who I had met on the previous day. Later, in conversation with my employer and some neighbours, I found out that the liquidation of the Łuków ghetto had occurred exactly at the time that I was getting my night's lodging and food in the different villages. Had I started my journey to Łuków a few days earlier I, too, might have lost my life. The railwayman, ignorant of my heritage, had unknowingly helped me at a most critical moment.

At the railway worker's, I was finally able to take care of my shoes. Days before I had arrived, while walking in the rain to that terrible scene in the town of Komarówka, my shoes had fallen apart, the soles separating from the tops. I had had no choice but to continue walking with what I had on, so I bound the shoes with a piece of wire and a rope I had found. Now I remembered how I used to watch Franiuk in the village of Sokoły as he went about his work, and I realized that I knew how to fix my problem. Franiuk used to cut out shoe bottoms from alder wood; then he shaped the soles, carving a concave hollow for the heel so the foot would rest on it comfortably. Around the top edges, he would make grooves with a chisel where he nailed the shoe

---

2 Partisans were members of resistance groups in Poland. For more information, see the glossary.

top to the wood. At Franiuk's, I had watched all this with youthful curiosity.

I badly needed shoes for the winter, as I had plenty of walking to do on the muddy and frozen ground, so I went about fixing my shoes with what I had learned. On the other side of the tracks, not far away from where I took the cow to pasture, there was a meadow, in the middle of which was a hollow where willow and alder trees grew. I chopped down a young alder tree and then cut a piece of wood that was sufficient for two wooden soles. Like Franiuk, I shaped the bottom parts, following the pattern of my old shoes, and then nailed the old leather top to my new wood soles.

When the season of taking the cow to the pasture ended, I was occupied with a variety of duties on the farm: chopping wood, cutting straw into chaff for the horse, threshing corn with a flail and grinding the wheat into flour. While performing all of these duties, I finally realized why the railwayman had taken me in. If he didn't deliver a certain amount of wheat to the Germans, as required by their orders – the so-called contingent – then he would not receive special permission to grind his grain in the community grinding mill.[3] To obtain flour to bake his bread, every week I would carry the threshed grain to his parents, who lived eight kilometres away, and grind it on a stone grinder. This meant that every week I walked eight kilometres along the tracks, carrying a sack of threshed grain that weighed about ten kilograms, and then walked another eight kilometres back with the flour.

On these journeys, I was aware of the great risk – if any passing army patrol or policeman had spotted me and interrogated me, my fate would have been sealed. My dangerous journeys with food were

---

3   Farmers were required to supply the German authorities with goods and produce, facing imprisonment or worse if they did not do so. On July 11, 1942, the Germans introduced a new law that advocated the death penalty for farmers who didn't provide the crop "contingent" to the German occupiers.

a sort of recapitulation; in the previous year, I had riskily returned to the Otwock ghetto with provisions, and now the danger was the same or, perhaps, even greater. I was fortunate that no one noticed me.

As if the work on the farm wasn't enough, the railway worker's daughter, Kasia, added to my burden. Kasia attended school in Łuków, and in class she mentioned that her father had a servant who threshed wheat by hand with a flail.

The teacher, a good friend of the railway worker, asked if I could be sent to him. Apparently he had a barn full of wheat still in ears and needed some grain. So I was sent to the teacher's place and for six days I threshed the wheat with the flail. There was a piano in the house, but no bed for me to sleep on. So, every evening, I carried a bunch of straw to the living room, spread the straw on the polished floor and slept on it there. After a week of this the schoolteacher told me to go back to my master, which was just fine with me. I never found out why my stay at the teacher's was cut short. Was it because I wasn't productive enough or because I littered the room with straw? In the end, it turned out to be somewhat of a humorous episode.

Despite the hard work, I was in many ways treated as an equal in my master's household, and it felt good. During the long winter nights, I had the opportunity to read Kasia's schoolbooks. She was my age. They also had two younger sons, Janek and Adam. Reading the catechism was especially important for me at that time and I also occupied myself by weaving baskets, preparing the proper materials from outdoors in advance. As I wove I sang all kinds of songs, among them Ukrainian songs, which were supposed to prove my heritage from the town of Dubeczno.

One day, the Ukrainian connection caught up with me. It turned out that there were Ukrainians in the service of the Germans at the railway station in the town of Łuków. Not far from the station, the Germans were holding a small group of Jews, whom they were using as slave labour, in a shack (this was after the liquidation of the ghetto). The Ukrainians were guarding the Jews, but in their free time some of them would go looking for adventure around the villages in the area. Across the road from our farm was a farm where two girls lived. They were popular with the "boys" from the railway station and the Ukrainians were often guests in their home. The neighbours knew of these visits. They also knew that I was a servant at the railway man's house.

Since my situation was so precarious, I had tried to create an alibi about myself so no one would suspect my origins. There's a saying that offence is the best defence, and that's exactly what I did. I talked a lot about the surroundings of Dubeczno, from where I was supposed to have come, and made much of my connections to the Ukrainian population there. Long before I knew that there were Ukrainians who worked at the railway station in Łuków, I continued with this charade of being a boy from Dubeczno, where the Polish and Ukrainian populations lived side by side, and where it was common for a Polish boy like me to use Ukrainian expressions.

One evening, while I was weaving a basket, a Ukrainian in a blue uniform rushed into the room along with a small boy from the neighbourhood who was his guide. When I saw him, a chill went down my spine. His tone, however, was friendly and he asked me where I came from because in the house where he was visiting with his friend, he had been told there was a Ukrainian servant next door. "So I came over right away," he said. "The more the merrier, and in these times we Ukrainians have got to stick together and make friends." I calmed down and in my already good Ukrainian told him that I was actually a Pole. The last thing I needed now was for anyone to find out I had been lying about anything. He asked me to sing something in Ukrainian since he had heard I had a nice voice. I started to sing a well-known Ukrainian song. He helped me out with his deep bass voice and, satisfied, went to join his "lady" across the road. I was relieved – my story was accepted as the truth and all was well.

At the time that the railwayman offered me work on his farm I was still using the assumed name Czesław Pinkowski. But I didn't have any documents to show who I was, and I knew that without Polish documents I wouldn't be able to survive. The question was where, and how, to obtain a Catholic birth certificate. In the meantime, my only "documents" were my knowledge of farm work and basket weaving, so I began to produce more of the latter in order to make myself useful. Most importantly, despite the cold weather, I did my everyday duties with enthusiasm. I cut straw for the horse, chopped wood, threshed wheat with a flail and carried the grain once a week to my employer's parents to be ground into flour.

In December there were heavy snowstorms and so sometimes I didn't go to grind the wheat. I would finish my regular work and return home to listen to Christmas carols, which the mistress of the house liked to sing. After listening closely for awhile, I would join in. In order to suppress my anxiety, when I was working outside, I sang all the songs I knew. Christmas was approaching and on Christmas Eve I also had to participate in decorating the Christmas tree. I should point out that when I was taking care of the cows in the various villages in the summer, there had never been any conversations about holidays or religious customs. Also, in the Ukrainian villages, I was in the company of my employers only when I had eaten with them; otherwise, I had slept on the hay in their barns. But in this house, I slept in the same room as the family and so, willingly or not, I had to participate in everyday life. I had to be careful in my conversations with Kasia, especially. When answering her questions, I had to be accurate – one wrong word could have created suspicion.

Another danger was that I was afraid that in my sleep I might say the wrong thing or make an unconscious slip; my dreams were scary, and one cannot control dreams. I was in a constant state of tension and afraid of everything. My employer's wife often spoke of customs in the area. For instance, the family names that ended in "ski" were deemed to be noblemen's names, and that accounted for some of the villagers' pride – they were able to claim that they were descended from noblemen. While I liked to listen to her talk, I was beside myself at the thought that one of these days something might happen to reveal who I was.

Although nothing dangerous happened to me then, in the beginning of the new year, in 1943, I experienced a number of close calls. On one nice, sunny day, when the newly fallen snow was already trodden down to form a firm surface on the roads, an army car drove slowly from the direction of Łuków and turned into the farmyard. An officer got out of the car. At first I thought that maybe someone had informed him that there was a boy at this railwayman's place and he had come to check out who I was. But as he stood in the farmyard I noticed that instead of a machine gun he was carrying a hunting gun.

My boss came out of the farmhouse. He seemed to know the officer because after some conversation with him he beckoned to me and told me to accompany the fellow on a hunt in the forest. It turned out that this German was a railway officer. Some of my anxiety abated, but I was still in shock. Here I was, going into the forest with a German officer who was carrying a gun. As we trekked through the forest, the snow was up to my knees and the only paths were the narrow ones beaten down by hares. The German pointed out the remains of a hare lying on the path where it had been caught in a wire snare. Most probably, dogs had eaten it. The entire time he kept talking and asking me questions, but although I understood him, I pretended not to. I was afraid to answer him in case I used a Yiddish word instead of a German one. Finally, he seemed to have become annoyed and waved for me to go home. I was pleased to see that he hadn't caught anything when he returned to his car.

It was a cold and bitter winter in 1943, and the snow and frost lay heavily on the ground. Likely because of the weather, the Nazis no longer needed the last of the remaining Jews that they had been keeping in the nearby shack for work, and they were going to be killed. Somehow, the Jews learned of their fate and, even more miraculously, they managed to escape from the shack behind the railway station. In the middle of the cold night there was a knock on the bedroom window; there they were – men and women, begging the railway man to permit them to stay the night.

In our farmyard there stood a big barn. The house, which had a large veranda, was situated to the left of it. The house consisted of a kitchen, which was also used as a dining room, and one big bedroom that doubled as a living room and in which we all slept. The other half of the house was used as the stable for the horse and the cowshed for the cow. At the side of the house was a little mound, built like a cellar, with a gate-like small door. In winter the mound served to keep potatoes and, in summer, it was used to hold milk and dairy products. We were already crowded in the one room, so some of the fugitives spent the night on the veranda, while others went into the mound. In the morning, after a fitful sleep, we woke up to find both places empty; there was no trace of the fugitives. They must have run into the nearby forest, and the wind had blown snow over their tracks.

As the winter progressed, something must have happened because I noticed that the railway man's attitude toward me began to change. He and his wife started to become impatient with me; I could feel it. In spite of my hard work on the farm, something was different in their everyday relationship with me. I wondered if he had discovered that I had told him some lies. It was a terrible dilemma for me, because I had nowhere else to go.

In the middle of March, while walking through the village on some errand, one of the farmers called out to me, "Aren't you the boy who works at the railwayman's place?" I told him I was only staying there through the winter and that soon I would be looking for another place as a herdsman. The farmer said, "If that is so, then after Easter, come to my place! I need a herdsman for the summer." I said that I would expect new clothing and shoes for my services. He introduced himself as Paul Siedlecki and we shook hands as we agreed on my wages.

Hence, by chance, I arranged another job for myself in the same village. Again I thought myself lucky that everything was turning out well. At the railwayman's, something was suspiciously wrong, and I was afraid that some day the situation could explode. I therefore didn't wait until the Easter holidays. On the first available occasion, I told him I was leaving. I felt indebted to this man; yet, after living at his house for almost six months and sleeping in the same room as the rest of the family, I knew I needed to leave.

It was on a rainy Saturday, near the end of March 1943, that I arrived at Paul's farm to take up my job as herdsman. I moved in with my belongings: some willow-wood branches and a half-finished basket. It turned out to be the last basket I would weave during my stay in the villages – at Paul's place I somehow didn't feel like weaving baskets anymore. Besides, later there was no time for it.

From the very beginning of my stay at Paul's place, I slept in the grandmother's room – she was called by the Polish word for grandmother, Babcia. When I started to sleep in her room, I showed her my prayer book. I told her it was from my first communion. Necessity forced me to lie and I continued to be "religious." Morning and night, before I went to bed, I knelt down and said my prayers. I gave every appearance of honestly believing in my faith. I also showed interest in the religious periodicals Babcia had on her bedside table. Sometimes I would discuss topics with her that I had read. She was happy to see me praying every day and reinforced my behaviour by saying what a good boy I was.

It was likely that the grandmother believed me, but it would have been much better if her son, Paul, had also been convinced. Soon after I arrived there, Paul arranged for me to look after a neighbour's cows, too. His name was Stanislaw and he lived across the road. It was too early in the season to take the cows to pasture, so I helped out on the farm. One day, I was told to deliver milk to the dairy station. I lifted the containers onto the horse-drawn cart, harnessed the horse to the cart and drove away. It was a cold, rainy day and to make matters worse it was very windy. While driving back home, the rain lashed against my face. To avoid the rain, I sat a little sideways and in this position I drove into the farmyard. A neighbour was approaching Paul's farm at the same time and must have noticed how miserable I looked.

I unhitched the horse, put away the milk containers and walked into the kitchen. The neighbour, Klimek, was in the midst of a heated discussion with my employer, which he ended with, "You can tell me what you want, but I am telling you he is a Jew!" With that, he walked out. I didn't know who he was talking about, and I wasn't sure if there was any danger here for me. I felt secure in my service at Paul's farm and had no reason to suspect anything. But from that day on, Klimek was at Paul's place every day and Paul soon became arrogant toward me, swearing at me for no reason, in an unbelievably crude fashion. But because he was similarly abusive to his own family – his wife and his daughter, Tereska – I wasn't on my guard. For some reason, he especially wanted to humiliate me, though, and his attitude became unbearable.

Paul hadn't mentioned anything about paying me for the additional work I had to do, so I thought I would arrange that payment with the other farmer on my own. I didn't know that for my service to Stanislaw, Paul would be the one to receive a fee, not me. Paul knew I had no documents and that I wasn't in any hurry to write home to Dubeczno, where I supposedly came from. It appeared that he didn't trust me. My previous work in the same village, for the railway man, hadn't made an impression on him.

It was possible that he suspected who I was. When he swore at me, many of the curses he used were distortions of abusive Polish expressions aimed at Jews. So why didn't I run away from this farm, from this village, like I had done previously? I still had no identity documents, and so I had nowhere to go.

My employer's arrogance was limitless. For instance, one day when we were working together, I was filling sacks of grain with a shovel for the spring sowing while he held the edge of the sack. After filling several sacks, I became tired and started to pour the grain more slowly.

Paul became angry and lashed out at me with vulgar words, saying that I was the bastard son of a father who had the poor taste of taking up with a Jewish prostitute in some attic. Was he trying to check my response? What could I do but shrug my shoulders and smile?

Paul and his friend Klimek hatched a scheme of which I wasn't to learn until a few months later from Paul's wife. One day, Paul and Klimek arranged to go to the forest to cut trees and I was to bring them lunch at noon. I thought nothing much of it, although I found this arrangement strange, especially when Klimek himself reminded me about it. The situation seemed cooked up. When that day came, I went to Paul's wife to ask for the lunch, as I had been told to do. To my surprise, she informed me that her husband had already taken food with him to the forest. She told me to do something on the farm instead.

It seemed like a mere change of plans in my daily work, but in reality, she had put a stop to the conspiracy her husband and Klimek were planning. Later that summer, Paul's wife revealed that they had planned to get me to the forest to pull down my pants and see if I was circumcised. According to Jewish religious tradition, all male infants are circumcised on the eighth day of their lives.[4] To find Jews who may have been hiding among the general Polish population, it was common practice to check whether the person had been circumcised.

Had they taken off my trousers, their suspicions would have been confirmed, in which case they would have dragged me to the police station in Łuków. Had they carried out that plan, I would have lost my life. Now, as I write about it, I surmise that the person who was against the plan was Paul's mother, Babcia, who was happy to see me praying every day. Luckily for me, Babcia was a force to be reckoned

---

4   As the practice of circumcision – the removal of the foreskin– was not the practice of non-Jews in Poland, a physical examination would have disclosed that Marian was Jewish.

with in that household. I assume that it was due to her intervention that the whole conspiracy came to nothing.

I have to also assume that to my employer I was probably worth more alive than dead. He was quite greedy, and it's possible that he was afraid of losing a good herdsman, whom he had obtained at a bargain price. Moreover, he was receiving an extra fee for me looking after his neighbour's cows. It could have been that Paul was afraid that had he checked me out and been mistaken about my identity, I would have been insulted by what he did and moved on. Consequently, he would have lost a herdsman as well as the fee from his neighbour.

Really, it's not important what prompted Paul to change his mind and not try to carry out the plan at some other point. The fact is that I continued to live. Nevertheless, I was wary of Paul and Klimek's intentions. Where one conspiracy ended, I imagined new ones that he could have arranged for me. One day, for example, I was working in a garden that was close to the farmyard. At lunchtime, while we were eating in the kitchen, a policeman biked into the farmyard, dismounted and came inside. I broke into a cold sweat when I saw him; I had to control myself and not show any sign of fear. I felt tension in the air. When the policeman showed up, I was alarmed, but Paul was happy to see him. "Zenek! My good friend, I didn't know you were in the police," Paul shouted. The big fellow, who looked more like a gangster than a policeman, explained, "It's my new job, and it's because of the Jews. I'm getting paid for the heads I catch and, on top of that, I get to take all of their possessions. It's common knowledge that Jews who are hiding have money or valuables. Give them to me! I line them up one behind the other in groups of three and mow them down with one bullet." Then he went on to brag about how good he was at recognizing Jewish traits. "It's enough for me to look into their eyes and right away I know if they're a Jew or not," he said proudly.

I felt hot, then cold, as he ranted on in a long monologue, sitting at the same table as me. They finished off several glasses of homemade potato vodka and then the subject changed. Zenek tried to enlist

Paul in his work, but he refused, saying, "I have a farm to look after." Although Paul turned down the position, he seemed very happy with the visit. At least he didn't have to drink alone while looking at himself in the mirror, as he sometimes did. Finally, the policeman left. He never showed up again, but there was a possibility that his arrival wasn't accidental. That day, I had noticed that Paul's wife had left the house in the morning to help her parents for the day on their farm, or at least that was what I had been told. It seemed to me that the policeman's visit with Paul, and his wife's absence all day, coincided in a dubious way. She never went to her parents again for the rest of the eight months that I stayed on their farm.

It was in this kind of everyday atmosphere, late in April 1943, that Paul approached me while I was chopping wood and said, "You know, the Jews in the Warsaw ghetto started an uprising. They captured a few wagons with ammunition and claimed that they could now fight for a whole year." I knew the conditions in the Warsaw ghetto, and I thought that what he was saying was either a product of his imagination or an exaggeration.[5] At the same time, I was curious about where he got this information. The way he mentioned it to me, however, was enough to put me on guard. He might have been testing me to see how interested I was in the subject. He often talked to me about Jews and made them subjects of vulgar, coarse jokes. I didn't know whether the Warsaw ghetto still existed. I thought it probably didn't because everybody knew that the Germans were liquidating the ghettos. Paul had told me that during the liquidation of the ghetto in Łuków a few women tried to hide in a large water tank. They were pulled out and shot on the spot. The death camps were no longer a secret, either. So how could there be an uprising in the Warsaw ghetto? Nevertheless, I didn't say a word.

---

5 The Warsaw Ghetto Uprising began on January 18, 1943, and continued until May 1943. On April 19, 1943, about 750 organized ghetto fighters launched an armed insurrection. The largest single act of violent resistance by Jews during the Holocaust, it was crushed on May 16, 1943. For more information, see the glossary.

At the end of April I once again started my occupation as a herdsman, taking the cows to pasture. At this time, my duties as a herdsman involved taking Paul's, Babcia's and Stanislaw's cows to pasture. Paul actually profited from the deal twice because every second week I would eat at Stanislaw's place. To me, it didn't really make any difference in which of the farmer's homes I ate. I was continuously worried about being discovered.

Paul liked to drink. On such occasions, he would invite company, which would increase my sense of danger. And no matter what they talked about, the conversation would always return to the subject of the Jews. What I heard was horrendous and macabre. In order not to listen, I found excuses to leave the room. Sometimes I asked my employer if I should take care of the horse, but he would already be a little drunk on his homemade vodka. I wouldn't wait for an answer, and would then leave the room. I would linger at my duties, combing the horse and checking the horseshoes while tears ran down my cheeks. At the same time, I was afraid someone might see me crying.

In the forest where I tended the cows, I felt normal and comfortable. There I met the boys from the village and made friends with them, and yet I was jealous of their carefree, happy lives. I was continuously thinking about how to obtain a Catholic birth certificate in order to ensure my future safety. I wondered how it would be possible to get that kind of document without help. In the previous year, when I was being driven to the railway station of Międzyrzec en route to the camp, the girl sitting next to me had begged the driver to help her obtain a Catholic birth certificate for herself and her sister. She was willing to exchange all of her valuables for that. Thinking of that incident, I was determined to obtain the necessary documents.

Although at first I didn't know how to go about it, somehow I figured out the appropriate steps to take. I started to imitate the behaviour of the other boys from the village, which included going to church on Sundays. The village life had its customs – Sunday services, aside from being a religious obligation, were also a social event. Therefore, in order not to draw any suspicion, I participated.

While going to church, I was able to find out what hours the church office was open, and at services, I would make myself very visible by sitting up at the front, so that everyone could see me. As I had anticipated, the women from the neighbouring homes started to whisper among themselves that Paul had a good boy for a herdsman. This talk probably reached Babcia's ears.

I took care of the cows seven days a week, so I occasionally sought help from Stanislaw. Stan, like Babcia, praised my piety. He would come to look after the cows for a few hours on Sunday mornings to fill in while I went to church. During mass, people would sing and ask God to perform miracles. This was precisely what I was thinking, and upon returning to the cows in the pasture I silently prayed and begged God to help me survive these terrible times. When I think about it now, I have to conclude that Providence guided me. I was spared from dangerous situations so often.

One day, I was told to run the cows on Stanislaw's field, which was located closer to town, instead of on the pasture in the forest of mixed trees where I usually went. It was already close to noon when two men with heavy clubs in their hands appeared out of nowhere and asked me, "Hey, have you seen any Jews running this way?" They were the *szmalcowniks*, the informants and blackmailers who thrived on Jewish misery and were similar to those I had seen operating in the city outside the ghetto. I told them I hadn't seen anyone and they ran off into the forest.

After awhile, I heard yelling and screaming, and a short time later I saw these bandits, together with German soldiers, strong-arming a Jewish family along the path – a couple with two children and another older couple who were probably the grandparents. Where had the Jews come from? The Łuków ghetto had been liquidated in October of the previous year, so they must have been hiding in the neighbourhood all this time. Maybe they had been caught while trying to change hiding places. I saw the Germans prodding them like cattle to the field, right next to where I was tending the cows.

The Jews were lined up in a row, as if posing for a family portrait. A series of rifle shots killed them on the spot.

It is for Your sake, that we are slain
all day long, that we are regarded
as sheep to be slaughtered.

Rouse Yourself; why do You sleep,
O Lord? Awaken, do not reject us
Forever!

Psalm XL: 23–24

How did I still manage to remain alive, when so many Jews were caught? I remembered again how in the previous year, at my uncle's house, I said I would rather be shot in the back and die instantly than go to the death camp at Sobibor. Now, standing in the field, while people were being slaughtered around me, my prediction almost came true. But I didn't want to be killed, no matter how. I wanted to live. The instinct of self-preservation turned my thoughts to life, and the sunny weather gave it a special meaning.

The cows wandered, grazing closer to the slope and the railway tracks. I pretended I was returning them to the field, but really I was prodding them away from this brutal scene, which became embedded in my mind. The Germans brought some workers from nearby houses to dig a pit for the bodies. The whole procedure swiftly became a spectacle: the clothes were taken off the murdered family and, to complete the degradation, one young woman even removed their underwear. I learned about that last event the next day, since everyone in the village was talking about it.

At lunchtime I herded the cows onto another road to come home but when I was trying to eat lunch, I vomited. I had to explain why I was sick to my surprised employers. I also told them that I would never again go with the cows to that place. From then on, for the rest of the summer, the only pasture I went to was the one in the mixed forest.

One beautiful July day, when my employer wasn't home, his wife gave me lunch and sat down at the table to talk. This was when she informed me of the real reason her husband and Klimek had wanted me to deliver lunch to them in the forest, that day way back in the spring. She asked if I would have been offended had they checked me out in this manner. "Because," she said, "Paul and Klimek suspect you are a Jew and, as you know, in these times it's very dangerous to keep someone on who might turn out to be a Jew. The penalty is death!" The conversation caught me by surprise, and I wondered what I was supposed to tell her. I had to say something, so I replied that had they taken off my pants like a little boy, I would have immediately left the forest and gone to Stan to be his servant. I would not have looked after their cows any longer.

Then she asked why I went to town so frequently and warned me that if I were to be stopped by the police, without any documents, they could take me for a Jew. Again, the dilemma confronted me: What should I tell her? I knew I had to make a good impression, so I laughed and said that I was going to town to the church and that sometimes I went to the post office to write a letter home to my mother. If by chance the police were to stop me, they could check in the Dubeczno municipality where I was born. My pretense of haughtiness must have worked, for I seemed to have persuaded her that I was telling the truth.

～

The forest where the cows grazed had various names among us herdsmen, depending on the location. The part where the railway tracks passed on their way to Siedlce from Brześć was called the Brześć pasture. Often, freight trains passed on these tracks. One day, an old villager by the name of Maciej was tending his cows with me. We called him Old Maciej, and he played a harmonica well. I knew him from before – he lived not far from the railway man's house and sometimes he showed up there. Maciej used to play the harmonica in the forest, and when we got together, he played and I sang.

One day, while performing our "concert," a freight train approached from the direction of Brześć toward Siedlce. From the distance, we could already hear rifle shots. When the train came closer, I noticed people in the freight cars and soldiers standing on the roofs with their rifles at the ready. Whenever someone stretched an arm through the slats of the freight car, a soldier fired a shot. It was a terrible and surreal scene. It seemed to me that these people, who had probably been cooped up in these freight trains for a long time, were stretching out their arms to the outside world to persuade themselves that they were still alive.

Although it was a hot day, a chill went up my spine and I broke out into a cold sweat. I knew that the same misfortune would have awaited me had I not run away from that horse-drawn cart carrying me to the Międzyrzec station. Old Maciej said, in a sad voice, "They're transporting them to be executed." He made the sign of the cross and started to cry. I was terribly affected by the dreadful destiny and misfortune of those people. But how much more secure was my life? I lived with people who had already proven that they were extremely suspicious of my identity – in my case, the best thing to do was to leave the cows in the pasture and run away, as I had before. But here I was, a year older, and still without any documents.

I knew that my only means of survival was to work on a scheme to obtain documents and so I stayed in the village, in spite of the danger, in order to carry out my plan to the end. Every freight train that passed by struck terror in my heart. My fear was immense.

About that time, for some reason, Paul had a disagreement with Stan. During July, the tension between them grew to such an extent that by the end of the month, Paul told me to stop tending to Stan's cows. From then on, to the end of the summer, I only looked after Paul's and Babcia's cows. Babcia also had a plot of land and, during harvest time when I came home for lunch, she would return with me to the field close to the farmhouse. She taught me how to scythe wheat in a gentle way and she became my friend and mentor. Since I believe in luck, I can say that what happened next was heaven-sent.

Many older folks like to talk, and this was certainly the case with Babcia. The old lady liked me, and she was always telling me all kinds of stories about the people in the village. I heard all the local gossip. There was one particular boy whom I often saw in the pasture, and I found out about his family from Babcia. According to her, he came from a "better family," a nobleman's family, and it turned out that it was he who, without knowing it, helped me to obtain my documents. If I believed in miracles, I would have to say that God sent Babcia to intervene on my behalf. Thanks to her storytelling, I obtained all the information I needed to get the birth certificate of a Polish Catholic boy, which in the most critical time helped me to survive. Although it took a long time, my plans finally started to take shape. I learned from the boy his birth date and the names of his godparents, and from Babcia I learned the other essential information about his family history that I would need.

It was November 1943. I hadn't taken the cows to pasture for some time. Instead, I was doing other chores on the farm, although Paul and I had agreed from the beginning, when I was first hired, that I would work for him only for the summer and would not stay at his place for the winter. He still owed me my payment of clothing and shoes, and I had had to wait until November to get it. For looking after Stanislaw's cows, Paul gave me two additional shirts.

Fortunately, by then I had worked out all the details in my scheme. What made it possible to carry out was the fact that the parish church wasn't located in the village where I was staying, but in town. Many small villages belonged to that parish. It was therefore impossible for the priest and his staff in the parish office to remember each one of the many boys from the villages. I was only waiting for the appropriate day to go to the parish office. One rainy day I told Paul that I was going to the post office to write to my mother and instead I went to the parish office in Łuków, taking with me my cherished savings from selling that camera from Komarówka all those months ago.

There, trembling with fear, I told the official that I needed my birth certificate. I stated "my" first and family name, then the names of "my" parents and godparents. She looked into the registry book and everything was correct. On an official sheet of paper, printed in Polish and German, she wrote down all the necessary information and told me to pay ten złoty. She also told me to go to the presbytery to see the priest for his stamp and signature. When I arrived there and opened the door, I saw the priest sitting at the table with two German officers. Confused and surprised, I didn't say anything. I just stood there. The priest looked at me and asked, "So what do you say?" At that moment I gathered my wits and uttered the common Catholic greeting, "Praised be the Lord Jesus Christ." I gave him the birth certificate and asked for his signature. The priest signed the document and told me to pay another five złoty, which I did.

Outside, there was a drizzling rain, but it didn't bother me. I was walking slowly and calmly. In my pocket I had a real Catholic birth certificate – in the name of Marian Domanski – that had a value far greater than the fifteen złoty I had paid. While walking, I thought of those two sisters with whom I had sat on that cart, riding to the death camp at what I now know was Treblinka. I wondered if they had also managed to run away and get Catholic birth certificates; I hoped that they had.

When I returned to Paul's I told him that I had written a letter home to my mother informing her of my return. I also told him that I wanted to leave in a few days. Paul was happy that he had had a servant for eight months for next to nothing, and I was relieved that I had managed to survive my stay in the village.

Dressed in my new clothes, I happily left the village. I left behind my imaginary name, which I had assumed the previous year in Sokoły. I also left my prayer book in Babcia's room. I simply forgot to take it with me, but in my new situation, it wasn't so necessary for me to have it. I was equipped with a document that gave me a new identity. I walked briskly and in the opposite direction, away from the town of Łuków.

In the evening, when I arrived in a new village, I visited the *soltys* and with his help obtained a night's accommodation. The next morning, I started looking for work as a farmhand. I now knew that village customs were to hire new help for the whole year, starting at Christmas time. I had also broadened my experience in farm work and could ask for good wages.

After several days of wandering to various villages, I found a farm to work on in the village of Ustrzesz. I was hired by a woman whose husband was in the resistance. He was seldom home because he was afraid of being arrested. That evening, as if by chance, her husband showed up, complimenting his wife on making a good decision by hiring me. He told me that my arrival had come just in time because he desperately needed help. Since I intended to stay at his place for a whole year, he said that I had to register with the *soltys*. In addition to the certificate I had, I would therefore also need a document from the registry of my previous place of residence.

Early the next morning, I left the farm in order to go "home" to get the special certificate. I had to go to the municipality located in a village called Brzeziny, not far from where I had worked at Paul's place. It was just on the other side of the tracks. Once again, I had to walk back toward Łuków. That night, I used the help of a *soltys* to find a place to sleep, and I arrived at the village where the municipal office was located the next day, before evening.

Although it was late, the office was still open. A clerk sat at the desk. For awhile I hesitated; I worried that he might know the family to which I was pretending to belong. The village where that family lived was just a few kilometres away, on the other side of the tracks. Could I take such a risk? I knew that I needed this document though, so, despite the danger, I approached the clerk and said that I was leaving the village for awhile and needed to be taken off the records of residence. He asked if I had some kind of identity document with me. I gave him the birth certificate. Without asking any questions, he filled out a form the size of a birth certificate, signed and stamped it, and charged me a fee of three złoty. The moment I walked out of that office, I was euphoric.

Now I had two documents – papers I had been dreaming of for more than a year – that would help save my life. That night, I went to the local *sołtys* to stay overnight at the village, and returned to my new employers the next day. Shortly afterward, I registered with the village administrator as a resident of Ustrzesz, employed as a farmhand.

According to German regulations, I also needed an identification card called a *Kennkarte*, and so I set about applying for that, too.[6] Since I needed a photo of myself, I went to a photographer in the nearby town of Radzyń-Podlaski. According to the birth certificate, I was a bit older, and I asked him to make me appear more mature in the picture. Of course I could not tell him why. He playfully scolded me, wagging his finger, but he did manage to make me look older than I really was. With the photos and the birth certificate, I applied at the municipal office of Radzyń for a *Kennkarte*. I was given a temporary document and told to pick up the *Kennkarte* from the village administrator in two months.

I had new documents and a new place of work, and from then on my identity would be like any other Polish boy.

In spite of my newly acquired legitimacy, I began to have certain misgivings about my situation. First of all, my new employer belonged to the resistance movement, although I didn't know to which political faction.[7] Nevertheless, if the police or the Germans were to

---

6 During World War II the Germans used *Kennkarten* as identity documents; they were issued to various groups and distinguished by colour: grey for Poles, yellow for Jews and Romas, and blue for Russians and other non-Polish Slavic peoples.

7 The Polish resistance was comprised of various political factions, the largest of

come to the farm looking for him and find me and check the authenticity of my documents, I wasn't sure what I would do. Even with my new identity, I preferred not to meet the authorities. So far so good, I thought, but I wasn't going to press my luck. I was afraid of being exposed as an imposter. It would have been quite simple for someone to discover that I wasn't the person whose name appeared on the birth certificate, especially given the special ways in which village activities were conducted.

For example, in order to obtain flour, the farmers used to grind their wheat in a community mill. During the occupation, as I mentioned before, the Germans made grinding a special privilege. To grind his wheat, a farmer needed to get a permit from the municipal office, where he would receive special coupons for food rations upon delivering a certain amount of grain – the "contingent" – to the Germans to keep their troops fed. These coupons were issued according to the number of family members. This worried me. What would happen if the family of the boy whose birth certificate I now had was denied a coupon for their son because residence records showed he no longer lived with them? Wouldn't they defend their right to the full number of coupons and go to the police to inform them that something suspicious was going on? The clerk of the municipality would then state that he himself filled out the form for the boy according to the birth certificate shown to him. So it would turn out that while the real person continued to live with his parents, an imposter had taken him off the registry. Tracing that incident, the police might discover

---

which was the Polish Home Army, or Armia Krajowa, formed in 1942 and loyal to the Polish government-in-exile in London. Another large, opposing group was the People's Army, which was a communist group loyal to the Soviet Union and run by the Polish Worker's Party. Other resistance groups were the National Security Corps (PKB) and the Polish People's Independence Action (PLAN) See glossary entries for partisans and Armia Krajowa for further information.

the rest of my activities, such as applying for a *Kennkarte*. Afraid of this possibility, I made the decision to leave Ustrzesz quickly.

One day, in January 1944, I told my employers that I didn't like working on their farm. The next day, I was back on the road, in search of a new job with another farmer. Only this time my walking wasn't "wandering" to the unknown because the temporary document and the birth certificate gave me courage, and I felt somewhat protected by my new identity. Within a short time, I found work with a farmer by the name of Albin, whose property was located on a hill on the outskirts of the village of Ossowa. It was about ten kilometres from the village of Ustrzesz and an equal distance from the town of Radzyń, where I had applied for the document. I showed the farmer my temporary document and told him I was awaiting my *Kennkarte*. I also mentioned my short stay in the village of Ustrzesz but, obviously, I didn't tell him the real reason I left my previous employer.

Albin was very pleased about my potential usefulness on his farm, and since the payment I asked for my services was a bargain for him, he took me on. At the very beginning of my employment there, before receiving my *Kennkarte*, I had a risky encounter with some armed men. One evening, a group of "partisans" came to the house, made themselves comfortable and started asking questions about whether the farmer had already delivered his contingent to the Germans. Albin said that he had done so. Then they started to ask about everybody in the house. Pointing to the farmer's wife, one of them asked: "Who is that woman?" The farmer replied, "This is my wife."

"And that girl?"

"This is my niece."

"And that boy?"

"This is my farmhand."

The partisan immediately declared, "This is a Jew." Looking at me, he said: "Come outside and we'll check you out, and if it turns out you are a Jew, you see that?" He showed me the end of the barrel of a rifle he was holding.

In that area, there were different factions of partisans: some were fighting the Germans and were really resistance fighters, while others were posing as partisans while robbing the local farmers. The terrible threat of being checked out was repeating itself, but this time at rifle point. Luckily, my employer, although he didn't know my background, came to my aid using every means to persuade them. "What are you doing, gentlemen?" he asked. "I know his family, who live not far from the town of Łuków. I myself brought him here. As you can see, this is a temporary document issued at the municipality office in Radzyń, where he applied for a *Kennkarte*."

In the meantime, Albin's wife had put a few bottles of moonshine vodka on the table and plenty of sausages. These "gentlemen" treated food and drink as serious business. Their visit was a strange one. It seemed to be for the sole purpose of checking me out, because they didn't take anything from my employer except what they ate and drank. As they left, they promised, "We'll be back!"

Shortly after that visit, I went to Ustrzesz, to the village administrator. He had my *Kennkarte* ready. I felt I didn't have to live in fear anymore. I didn't register with the village administrator for residency at Albin's place, and because of that, no one could find me. I had applied for the *Kennkarte* first. I was still not sure what would happen if the real person applied for the document and submitted the same birth certificate, but I felt secure enough to stay in Ossowa.

Although I never again saw that group of partisans who tried to check out my identity, several other groups of partisans passed through our locality. Once, while a group of partisans was taking food from Albin, one of them snatched away my new pants for which I had worked so hard at Paul's. Another time, one of them tried to persuade me to go with them. I hesitated because I was suspicious of their intentions.

At the farm, my duties were to look after four horses and four cows; later I learned to milk the cows. This skill added to my value in my occupation as a farmhand. Kazia, Albin's niece, profited from my work. I filled in for her by milking the cows when she went to church on Sundays or out with her girlfriends. I no longer had to go to church to prove my piety.

I had a short-lived romance with Kazia. She was about two years older than me. She looked like a typical peasant girl, with large breasts, to which I was attracted, like most fifteen-year-old boys would be. When we were alone, my hand automatically reached toward her bosom. Since she didn't show any displeasure, I became a little bolder each time. Finally, Kazia reproached me, saying, "You are too young for these things." I didn't quite understand what she meant, but I was offended and the short romance came to an end.

The village of Ossowa was at a fair distance from the railway station. Nevertheless, from time to time, smugglers from Warsaw would turn up there in order to trade goods. I was astonished to see how similar their way of trading was to the way mine had been. Just as I used to trade goods from the ghetto for food, these people brought with them all kinds of goods that they exchanged for foodstuffs – the only difference was that they did it on a much larger scale. The people from Warsaw lugged huge bundles, which they exchanged for provisions like lard or meat products. My boss was often visited by a married couple who were traders from Warsaw. They had befriended him and when they traded in the neighbourhood, they would stay overnight at his farm. Other traders would turn up there too, and all of them claimed to have come by short-distance local trains, which were not searched by the German police. As a punishment for transporting large amounts of foodstuff, the Germans were sending people to the concentration camps.

One afternoon, one of the smugglers who used to get food from Albin arrived shaken and scared after what had happened to him on the way from the train. Instead of walking to the farm on the usual road, he took a shortcut through the fields and bushes. There, he was stopped and questioned by a group of Polish resistance fighters. He explained that he had just arrived from Warsaw and intended to buy some products from farmers. "Are you a Jew?" one of the partisans asked. He denied it and repeated that he had come to the village, like many others, to obtain some food. Finally, one of them ordered him to pull down his pants. Seeing that he wasn't circumcised, they let him go. Thus, he arrived, upset, at Albin's place.

Albin didn't have children of his own. Still, he was as greedy as if he had a large family. Because he had a fairly sizeable farm, there was a lot of work to be done, and in the spring my responsibilities increased. I can say for sure that of all my work in different villages, at Albin's farm it was the most difficult. Moreover, he didn't deal honestly with me. I was hired mainly to look after the cows and to only help out on the farm from time to time, but he disregarded the agreement and loaded me mainly with farm work. As it happened, I didn't mind.

I was grateful for his help in intervening when the partisans tried to take me outside and check me out – he had unknowingly saved my life. I therefore tried to carry out even the heaviest work willingly, like cleaning the manure out of the cowshed, which was mixed with straw and trampled by the cows during the winter, or scything the grass all day long.

When I had worked in the village near Łuków on Babcia's part of the field, I had used a scythe to harvest the grain and she gathered it. The work took only an hour or two, daily, and it was a pleasant diversion. At Albin's I had to cut the grass in the meadow together with the other cutters all day long. Although I was used to hard work, I could not do it at the same speed as the others, and I usually remained far behind. Albin didn't spare me work such as this, which was beyond my strength. Yet, I still felt greatly obliged to him.

In the summer of 1944, the Soviet Red Army was moving quickly toward the western part of Europe, and at the end of July, at harvest time, the Lublin area was liberated from German occupation. In Albin's village, Soviet soldiers arrived through the fields and farmyards. When they came to Albin's farmyard, I was sitting by a steamer, making moonshine (homemade alcohol). It didn't take the soldiers long to find out what was in the steamer. I brought them some cups and they drank the warm moonshine until the kettle was empty.

With the Lublin district liberated, I found that I could go anywhere I wished, now that I was a free man. But where would I go? I knew that not one member of my family or any distant relative was alive in Poland. From my own experience, and from what I had heard, I thought that no Jews had survived. Therefore, for all my cleverness and resourcefulness, I had adapted myself to village conditions and the work there. I didn't know anything else.

Starting Over

I was a little confused and didn't know what to do or where to go. The war action on Polish territory had moved on from our area toward the Vistula River. Subsequently, the Warsaw uprising took place at the beginning of August 1944. In the Lublin area, where I was, the underground Polish Home Army (Armia Krajowa, or AK) was organized to commence the uprising and assist in the liberation of Warsaw. The day before they planned to march toward Warsaw, the Soviet army began to encircle the place where the AK had concentrated, but after days of fighting between the AK and the Germans, the Soviets didn't intervene. Soviet commander Marshal Konstantin Rokossovsky and his army were standing by on the other side of the Vistula, watching the Germans butchering the people in the city, which instilled anger in the population.[1]

With Lublin liberated and the war still going on, I decided that I might as well remain in the village. I stayed with Albin until the end of the year and in January 1945, I started looking for new employment. I returned to the village of Ustrzesz, intending to visit the farmer I

---

1 By October 2, 1944, the attempt at liberation had been crushed and the results were devastating: more than 150,000 civilians had been killed and more than 25 per cent of Warsaw had been destroyed. Rokossovsky had followed Stalin's orders to deny support to the AK uprising. For more information, see the glossary.

had left after applying for the *Kennkarte*. The farmer's wife was home alone again. It turned out that the Germans hadn't seized the farmer, despite his involvement in the underground. After Poland was liberated from the Germans, it was the Polish Communist regime that arrested him for belonging to the AK, which was considered a right-wing group.[2] The story took me by surprise.

I looked for jobs in many other villages and finally found a farmer who needed my services. His farm was close to the town of Radzyń. I was already a qualified farm and field worker, so I demanded fair wages for a boy my age with my experience – one hundred kilograms of grain and one hundred kilograms of potatoes per month. When I said that I wanted everything in cash, based on the price for that quantity of produce, the farmer agreed. I now had an income and was happy with my new employment arrangements. However, I didn't like his attitude. Before the war, he had been the *wójt*, or mayor of a rural municipality. It seemed that the position left its mark in terms of the way he dealt with people, and certainly with me. Nor did I appreciate the manners of his wife. For instance, I was served food at a different time than my employers and so I ate alone. When they had guests, which was almost every weekend, I couldn't enter the house. This arrangement seemed bizarre to me.

Although Poland had been fully liberated since March 1945, some groups of resistance fighters remained. I guessed that my employer must have had connections with them because they frequently came to his house at night and sat in his bedroom, talking for hours. These partisans were called the "men of the forest."[3] On one occasion, when

---

2   After the Armia Krajowa failed to liberate Warsaw, the communist Polish Workers' Party began to gain support in Poland, and, under Stalin's direction, lobbied for control of the country. On January 1, 1945, the communist Polish Committee of National Liberation became the central governing force of Poland.

3   The *leśni*, or men of the forest, were informal groups of partisans formed during World War II. Though some followed the direction of the Polish Home Army, many were independent, with no particular political affiliation.

my employer sold a young cow at the market, the group came at night and, as per usual, sat in the bedroom talking while I slept in the kitchen. As they were leaving, they woke me up. One of them pointed a machine gun at me and demanded to know where my employer kept the money he had received for the cow. How was I to know? I didn't realize that this was their idea of a joke. After frightening me badly, they went back to the bedroom, talked for awhile, and left. The next morning, while giving me breakfast, the farmer's wife informed me that the partisans had taken all the money. At the time I believed her, because the year before, at Albin's place, such people had robbed me of my new pants, an incident I had told her about.

One morning, a woman from a nearby farm came by, shouting, "They've killed the Jews in Wohyń!" She didn't say who had done it, although she described exactly how it had been done. In the little town of Wohyń, close to the town of Radzyń-Podlaski, lived several Jewish families who had returned home after the war. One evening, the group of Jews was rounded up and herded into one room – men, women and children. They were all shot.[4] While shooting, the bandits threw the bodies on the ground, one on top of the other. One boy fell down and the other bodies were thrown on top of him. After the bandits finished the execution and left, the boy pulled himself out from under the corpses and ran to a neighbour's house, where a woman took care of him, washed him and changed his clothes. Listening to these details put me in a state of shock. I kept standing up and sitting down, and I couldn't finish my breakfast. It made me wonder how, just a few kilometres away, there were Jews about whom I knew nothing. I also thought about the night visits of the "people of the forest." Were they the ones responsible? It was difficult to know. There were so many political factions at the time.

---

4 Either the Polish underground or the Armia Krajowa was responsible for killing seven Jews in Wohyń. This wasn't an isolated incident – Jews were being killed by various groups of Polish partisans throughout the Radzyń-Podlaski area, and many Jews left the Lublin area to seek safety elsewhere.

At the beginning of May 1945, I came across an article in a newspaper that said 50,000 Jews had survived in Poland.[5] Upon reading that, I said to myself, "I am one of those 50,000 Jews." From that day on, I was no longer interested in working on a farm. I decided to leave and didn't even ask for my last month's wages. With his bad manners, this *wójt* fellow didn't deserve the kindness of any notice from me. Early one morning, instead of embarking on my usual farm duties, I put on my good clothes, wrote a goodbye note and left it on the table. I went straight from the farm to the railway tracks and walked in the direction of Lublin. It was the last time I took this route, and it was the day I left my occupation as a farmhand and the way of life connected to it.

I followed the tracks and wandered into a town called Parczew, located close to the railroad. It was there, in a small store in the town of Parczew, that I had an amazing surprise; or perhaps one can say that this was the second surprise – the first one was reading that 50,000 Jews had survived. I heard a young girl in the store speaking to someone in Yiddish! I engaged her in conversation, mentioning the place where I had come from. Surprised, she asked, "You walked from as far away as Radzyń-Podlaski?" Her father soon arrived and we talked for awhile. He asked why I had stayed in the villages for so long, instead of going somewhere safer, like a kibbutz.[6] After all, the Lublin area had been liberated nine months earlier. I explained my reasons and showed him my *Kennkarte*, describing how I was able to obtain it. During the conversation, I told him about how I criss-crossed across Poland – starting from Otwock, near Warsaw, to the village Kozaki, near Dubeczno, then escaping the transport carry-

---

5   Out of a pre-war population of 3,500,000 Jews in Poland, an estimated 50,000 to 120,000 survived the Holocaust.

6   A kibbutz is a collectively owned farm or settlement in Israel; many existed before Israel became an independent state, and many post-war Jewish refugees sought to build new lives on these collectives.

ing me to Treblinka, and subsequently heading once more to Łuków and then in the opposite direction, to Radzyń-Podlaski. Of course, he commended my resourcefulness and asked my real name. He wrote it down, and gave me food and money to buy a train ticket to Lublin.

I arrived in Lublin and at the station I saw people with suitcases going to a train, so I followed them and found myself hopping on a freight train to Warsaw. After two days, I arrived in Warsaw. The train stopped at the Praga station on the south side of the river because the main station had been damaged. From there, people walked to Warsaw across a wooden bridge over the Vistula. I went along with them. They all had a definite destination, but I didn't know what to do next. The scene was terribly depressing – half-ruined houses stood here and there amidst the rubble. After walking a little, I turned back to the Praga station, wondering where to go. The distance from Praga to Otwock was only twenty-eight kilometres, but just thinking about that place made me recoil. Too many unpleasant and painful memories that I wanted to forget were connected with it. I couldn't return to Otwock.

Having discovered that by hopping on freight trains I could travel freely, I continued my wandering, looking for a place to live. From Warsaw I went to Krakow, then to Lodz, where I went to the office of the Central Committee of Polish Jews – which everyone called the Jewish Committee – and asked for help.[7] I told them that I had recently left the villages where I was hiding during the war, and I needed a place to live. It seemed, though, that the Jewish Committee wasn't yet fully established to be able to help people like me. The woman at the desk repeated what the man in Parczew had already told me and said, "A boy like you should join a kibbutz." She proceeded to elaborate on

---

7   The Central Committee of Polish Jews was established in 1944 and was officially recognized as the highest administrative body of Polish Jewry. The Central Committee, which sought to reconstruct post-war Jewish life in Poland, received funds from the Polish government, as well as from the American Jewish Joint Distribution Committee (JDC).

all the advantages of such a step. But I didn't want to continue doing farm work and I had expected something more of her, at least a word of encouragement and an interest in my present situation. It's possible that it was her cold attitude that set me against the city of Lodz. It seemed there was no help for me from that source, so I left the office.

I found myself wandering on Piotrkowska Street, the main thoroughfare of the city. Here in Lodz I was a stranger and I wondered what to do. Jews who had survived were establishing themselves in the city or elsewhere and were talking of going west, to the Polish recovered territories – cities such as Wrocław and Wałbrzych.[8] Having been denied the help I needed, I promised myself never again to ask any institution for assistance. I still had my *Kennkarte* and my birth certificate, my only two documents, with somebody else's surname.

I eventually decided to stay on in Lodz, even though my first impression had been negative. I tried different jobs and found work in a basket-making shop. I certainly knew how to weave baskets, but the owner could not provide me with a permanent place to stay, so I had to leave. Once again, I found myself on the street. Then, walking down Piotrkowska Street, I noticed a shoemaker's shop. I entered it with some trepidation and told the owner that I wanted to learn the trade. In the course of our conversation, I told him about my work in the villages. The shoemaker accepted me as an apprentice. He offered to feed me and to let me sleep in the shop at night. Under his careful tutelage, I acquired professional shoemaking skills.

In the beginning of August 1945, I began to doubt whether being a shoemaker was a fitting occupation for me. I didn't see any hope of improving my life through that work. The war had interrupted

---

8 Polish recovered territories, also known as the Western and Northern territories, encompassed previously German areas in Western Pomerania, Lubusz Land, Silesia, Gdańsk and Warmia and Masuria. Polish and Ukrainian civilians were encouraged to live in these areas, from which most of the ethnic German population had been expelled.

my schooling and I gave some thought to furthering my education. Finally, I said goodbye to the shoemaker and decided to leave Lodz. I travelled by train to Wrocław and from there to Wałbrzych. I couldn't find a job in Wałbrzych that would enable me to simultaneously attend school, so I returned to Wrocław.

During this time, trains still did not arrive and depart on schedule. Sometimes I had to wait for a very long time for a train to my next destination. I ate at temporary shelters, which had been set up at railway stations for people displaced by war. During one such waiting period at the Wrocław station, I met some people who were going to the town of Rychbach, formerly known as Reichenbach.[9] I accompanied them there. I liked the town; it felt friendly and full of opportunity, and so I settled there. It had previously belonged to Germany and after the war it was in the Polish recovered territories. So there I was, in a new town, under new circumstances, having to adjust all over again to completely new conditions.

～

The adjustment to town life on my own, without any help from adults, was extremely difficult, especially since I had no knowledge of how to settle into the everyday kind of things that most people take for granted. I needed to find a place to live, to arrange to return to school and to adjust to normal life. I finally found work in a factory and I registered to attend evening school at the same time.

In addition to working and studying, I attended meetings of Jewish youth groups, and some of them urged me to join them and leave for Palestine. However, I wasn't ready for such a drastic deci-

---

9 Located in the southwest of Poland in the area of lower Silesia, Reichenbach was German before the war but became a recovered territory after and its name was changed to Rychbach. In 1946 the town was re-named Dzierżoniów, in honour of Jan Dzierżon, a famous Polish scientist. Between 1945 and 1948, the town had a large Jewish community of more than 10,000 Jews.

sion. Besides, I had my own private dreams. Of course, news about the post-war murder of Jews on the trains and in some small towns reached Rychbach.[10] Many Jewish survivors who had returned home to find out about the fate of their families and friends were murdered by Poles who had taken possession of their houses and belongings. Others were killed by Nazi-inspired antisemitic gangs. In July 1946, when news of the pogrom in the city of Kielce reached our town, several Jews panicked and left for Palestine.[11] However, Rychbach was distant from those places and there were no anti-Jewish excesses. Besides, after surviving the years of German occupation the way I did, I was no longer scared, and I hoped that these anti-Jewish actions would soon pass.

Slowly, I began adjusting to normal life. In my desire to free myself of the memories of my terrible years of hiding, the first thing I did was revert to my original family name, Finkelman. But life had some new surprises for which I wasn't prepared. I soon learned that under the name Domanski, rather than Finkelman, I would have a much better chance of achieving my goals.

A proper solution to this problem would have been to follow those who decided to leave for Palestine, but I preferred to establish myself in the land where I was born. In Rychbach (later, in 1946, the town was renamed Dzierżoniów), time passed quickly. During a photogra-

---

10 Antisemitism continued to flourish in Poland after 1945, and atrocities committed against the Jews resulted in more than 1,000 deaths between 1945 and 1947. Attacks on trains and in train stations were common and involved collaboration amongst passengers. Other pogroms occurred in towns such as Rzeszów, Tarnów and Sosnowiec.

11 In Kielce, where about 250 Jews lived after the war (the pre-war Jewish population had been more than 20,000), riots broke out after a false account of a young Polish boy kidnapped by Jews emerged. In retaliation, police arrested and beat Jewish residents, which incited a mob of hundreds of Polish civilians, who violently attacked and killed forty Jews, while police stood by.

phy course I was taking, I met a boy my age named Kazik Dąbal who, like me, had spent the years of German occupation hiding in villages somewhere in eastern Poland. He now goes by the name Edmund and lives in Israel; we have kept in touch over the years and remain close friends.

~

When I attended school in Dzierżoniów, I got to know a group of boys from the nearby town, Piotrolesie. They were all younger than me and some of them lived in an orphanage. I visited them from time to time to play soccer. During one visit, I met a girl who lived with her mother and two younger sisters in Radzyń-Podlaski. During the occupation her mother had worked in the office of a co-operative called Spolem under a false name, with "Aryan" documents. I also made friends with a boy several years younger than me who lived in the orphanage.

One day, in the fall of 1946, I arrived on my bicycle in Piotrolesie to play soccer with my friends. During a break, I asked one of the boys where he came from. He answered that he was from Wohyń. Upon hearing this I became intrigued and inquired, "Is that the Wohyń not far from Radzyń-Podlaski?" The boy confirmed that it was that place, and I suddenly was moved by the memory of the tragic event that I had heard of there. I told the boy, briefly, of the massacre of several Jews in that town at the end of February or beginning of March of 1945, in which only one boy was saved. My new acquaintance looked at me and said, "I am that boy, and my uncle, with whom I lived, was among the murdered people." After the game ended, we parted, not saying any more to one another. At that time, nobody wanted to be reminded of these tragic experiences. Later, while I was writing these memoirs, I found an extract pertaining to the boy from the orphanage in the Jewish Historical Archives in Warsaw. The boy was Mendel Cienki, born in 1932 in Wohyń.

The autumn weather was often not favourable for bike riding or playing soccer, so I stopped visiting the boys in the nearby town. Later, I lost all contact with them. During my years in Dzierżoniów, while attending high school, I dreamed of becoming a pilot. I knew from experience that dreams can become reality – one only had to take the steps to make it happen. So instead of finishing high school, I sent an application to the Military Recruiting Board in Dzierżoniów, expressing my wish to join the air force and become a pilot. For over a year, I inquired about the status of my application at the office of the military department. Finally, they promised to send me to an air force flying school.

Full of hope and trust, I waited for news of my acceptance. But unfortunately, at the end of 1949, I was sent to the air force technical school in Bemowo, near Warsaw, instead of flying school. My disappointment was great, and became even greater later on, when I became the butt of racist jokes at my new school. That happened when my surname, Finkelman, was recognized as Jewish. A particularly malicious boy named Waldek made my life very miserable. Before enlisting, he had been studying to be a tailor. In the evenings, in our dormitory, he would bully me and his taunting became worse as time went by. One day, when I could no longer stand it, I hit him with a stool. A commotion ensued and an officer of cultural-political affairs arrived to investigate. He delivered a lengthy lecture on the evils of racial discrimination and after that the jeering stopped.

After studying aerial photography and photogrammetry for one year, I graduated with distinction and was posted to the air force headquarters laboratory in Warsaw. There, the commanding officer of my section offered to send me on a one-year course to become a navigator in a bombing squad. But ever since the antisemitic incidents at the Bemowo school, I had lost interest in pursuing a military career. Since I was a volunteer, I could resign from military service, which I did after working for one year in the laboratory. So after two years of service, I returned to civilian life.

Realizing that all my efforts to achieve a military career in the

Polish air force had turned out to be no more than a young man's fantasy was a difficult blow. I hadn't taken into consideration the continuing reality of antisemitism. The psychological distress that I had experienced at Bemowo had resulted in me giving up my pursuit of a military career. My first reaction was to think about immigrating to Israel. However, at that time, and during the following five years, there was no possibility of emigration from Poland.[12] I was a civilian again and I had to find a place to live and to work.

~

When I was in the air force in Warsaw, in 1951, I decided to visit my hometown, Otwock. Walking in the direction of the house where I had once lived, I saw the pine trees I had climbed many years ago. Everything looked as it did before. Some pine trees seemed to have lost their bark and then I remembered that I myself had cut the bark off with an axe in 1940 to use in the stove for heating. Looking at these clipped trees, and at the house now occupied by other people, I was filled with memories and emotion. I turned and ran away, intending to leave that town again. However, when I was close to the railway station I continued to go further on Warszawska Street. I decided to visit Dłuska Street and search for the house where Juda Cytryn had lived.

Before I got there, at the corner of Warszawska and Kościelna Streets, I met the local parish priest, Father Wolski. During our short conversation he told me of a woman from his parish by the name of Waclawa Gobka, who lived at 61 Reymonta Street. She had hidden the former milk distributor, Pinaj Grinsztajn, after the liquidation of the Otwock ghetto. I was pleasantly surprised to hear that there were Otwock residents who had saved Jews during the war.

---

12 The Communist regime in Poland restricted legal emigration between 1949 and 1956.

~

Dzierżoniów, where I had lived before joining the air force, had ongoing Jewish activities and somewhat resembled a pre-war Jewish shtetl (small town). I liked the place and in 1952, after ending my service in the army, I returned there. I successfully completed a test in professional photography and started to work there as a photographer. I encountered all kinds of people while working in that field, and I felt uncomfortable introducing myself by my original family name. Although the war against Nazism had been won, many racial prejudices still existed in Polish society, so in 1952 I reverted to the Polish name Domanski, the name on the birth certificate I had used during the German occupation. Many others Jews did the same. I was also busy preparing for studies at the University of Wrocław's Faculty of Law, but I dropped out of university after two years, preferring a career in photography.

In 1954 I opened a studio, first in a small town near Wrocław and then in the city of Wrocław. My photography business in the centre of Wrocław was well established, and I was doing well financially. The studio was on the same street as the Wrocław opera house and the Jewish theatre, and I often attended performances at both venues. I became known for the quality of my work, or maybe it was just good timing, and the number of my clients quickly multiplied. I had to hire a helper and a student. I ventured into new professional areas, such as industrial photography and photo engraving for government firms.

Time passed quickly. In 1963, I completed a professional exam in general photography and was awarded the degree of Master Photographer. That same year I met a beautiful young lady named Cesia. We got married and the following year we had a daughter, whom we named Beata-Romana. Many wonderful things happened that year, one after the other. I received an invitation from Edmund, my friend in Israel, to visit him. I accepted, and it turned out to be a marvellous trip. I travelled by train from Warsaw to Vienna, then further on through Greece and into the capital city of Athens. There, in Port Pireus, I boarded a steamship to Haifa. The ship stopped for a short while in Cyprus, and the passengers had a chance to visit the island and shop. It was November 22, 1963. I was enjoying a cup of Arabic coffee in one of the coffee houses together with other passengers when we heard about the assassination of the President of the United States, John F. Kennedy, on the radio.

My friend Edmund met me in Haifa and we travelled to his home in Jerusalem. I then returned to Haifa to visit Hershel Finkelman, my father's cousin whom I had first visited in Otwock when I was four years old. This cousin had immigrated to Palestine during the 1930s and, before I had left Poland, I found out his address. From him, I got the address of another cousin, Shlomo Finkelman, and I visited him, too. He lived in Rishon LeZion. He told me that during the war he had joined the Polish army under General Anders in the USSR and was thus able to leave the Soviet Union with them.[13]

I also visited the Yad Vashem Museum in Jerusalem, looking for traces of surviving Jews from Otwock. I was given several memoirs from my hometown and while reading them I came upon the name of Maria Weczer-Tau, a former classmate of mine in Otwock. (Later, I found her in a town in Israel.) In her memoir she wrote that she survived the years of the occupation in Otwock for some time by hiding with a Catholic family. She mentioned that Juda Cytryn's siblings, Baila and Szmulek, lived in the Otwock ghetto on Dłuska Street in the same house as her and had also survived the genocide. In 1946, they had left for Palestine.

In her memoir she also praised the "just" Poles from our town: Karol Chlond, Secretary of City Hall; and fathers Ludwik Wolski and

---

13 General Anders was a Polish army officer who formed and led a large force of Polish exiles in the Soviet Union after June 1941. For more information, see the glossary.

Jan Raczkowski, both of whom, after the liquidation of the Otwock ghetto, provided Catholic documents to a number of Jewish children. Her next tale was shocking. During the liquidation of the ghetto, many children spent several days in different hiding places. When they came out, hungry and thirsty, some of the women who were caretakers caught them and handed them over to the Germans, receiving a monetary reward for each Jewish child.

I travelled around the beautiful land of Israel during my short visit, trying to learn as much about the country as I could. After returning to Poland, I tried to expand my photographic business by venturing into new areas of technical photography and also by working for different government firms. As time went on, from 1964 to 1968, my business became very prosperous; nevertheless, I eventually decided to leave Poland.

Leaving Poland

I had tied my fate to the land of my birth, and I had never considered leaving Poland. I thought that having been born in Poland and raised in Polish culture, and having lived everyday life as a Polish citizen, I had the right to consider myself a Pole, albeit of Jewish descent. My opinion was that neither religion nor race made any difference. Consequently, I thought I had the right to be recognized as a Polish citizen with full rights. But my opinion changed, partly due to events in Poland between 1967 and 1968.

During that period, the conflict in the Middle East became a point of contention in Poland. The Arab nations' policies, which included closing the Gulf of Aqaba and refusing to recognize the Jewish state's right to exist, was supported by the Soviet Union and its satellite countries, including Poland. In June 1967, in a war known as the Six-Day War, Israel launched a pre-emptive strike against the larger Arab armies that were gathered on its borders. At the same time, it conquered a number of territories: the Golan Heights, the Sinai Peninsula, Judea, Samaria and East Jerusalem. Israel's victory was met with a range of reactions among the Polish population. The small number of Jews who were still living in Poland either openly or covertly manifested their pride and satisfaction in the Six-Day War. The Polish Communist regime, however, following the USSR's policy of backing the Arab states, condemned Israel and, within a few days, broke diplomatic ties with Israel.

It should be understood that I wasn't alone in deciding to leave Poland during this time – thousands of Polish citizens of Jewish descent left as well, especially after an infamous anti-Jewish speech given by Władysław Gomułka, first secretary of the Polish Worker's Party (the Communist Party) on June 19, 1967.[1] His speech described the Jews living in Poland – because they were siding with Israel – as a potential fifth column (secret collaborators) whom he claimed were endangering world peace and, at the same time, the security of Poland. His speech instigated an antisemitic campaign. All sections of the government, especially the nationalists headed by General Moczar, started to attack the "Zionists," who became synonymous with Jews.[2] The Communist government authorities organized gatherings and public meetings in factories and other places of work to condemn Israel. Jews were subsequently fired from positions of responsibility in various industries and an antisemitic purge began in the Polish army and in the government.[3]

In a disturbing repetition of events two decades earlier, a Jewish Section was created within the Ministry of Internal Affairs to document the "racial purity" of citizens – by the mid-1960s, the ministry had mobilized a large department to create, meticulously and speedily, a registration of those inhabitants of Poland who had at least one Jewish ancestor within the last three generations.[4] The anti-Zionist

---

1 For more information on Władysław Gomułka, see the glossary.
2 General Mieczysław Moczar was minister of the interior, head of the security police and leader of a faction of nationalist, militant partisans within the Communist Party.
3 Approximately 9,000 Jews lost their jobs during these "purges."
4 The Jewish Section of the ministry's Department of Nationalities, staffed by more than two hundred employees, created a card index that effectively registered all Jews in Poland, including Poles who had converted to Judaism or who had married Jews, as well as those that had any Jewish relatives. During the height of the antisemitic purges in Poland, this list was used to identify and target Jews in the workforce, expelling them from positions in the public service and academia.

attacks and the efforts to find an imagined enemy became even stronger after the events of March 1968, when the government banned a theatre performance of *Dziady* (Forefathers' Eve) in Warsaw.[5] Articles, unscrupulous in their anti-Jewish rhetoric, appeared in the press and a mass campaign with the slogan "Zionists to Zion" began. What the slogan actually meant was that Jews were not welcome in Poland and that they should go to Israel. By using all types of propaganda and persecution methods, such as firing Jews from their jobs, they forced people to emigrate.

Thus, between 1968 and 1972, more than 20,000 people left Poland, among them students, intellectuals and scientists. I, too, began to discuss with my wife the possibility of leaving Poland. Although I had changed my family name to one that sounded typically Polish, in general I didn't hide my Jewish ancestry, which was obvious to those who knew me, including the photographers in Wrocław. They also knew that my business was performing very well, something they could not match. Naturally, some of them envied me. In 1968, at a time when antisemitism was accepted, two of my "friends" in the photography business took advantage of the atmosphere by trying to get me in trouble with the authorities. They made me a target of an investigation by a special "committee" that intended to do a financial audit of my establishment and to make sure my studio was proper for the kind of work I was doing. This was preposterous. In reality, I didn't have to worry, because everything was in order. I also knew that this was a conspiracy against me, as I had learned about their plans be-

---

5   Originally written in 1824 as a poem by Adam Mickiewicz, the play was banned for its supposed anti-Soviet elements because it focused in part on Polish patriotism under early-nineteenth-century Russian rule. Initial protests against the ban by the Warsaw Writer's Union triggered large student protests on university campuses across Poland. The Polish government responded with military action under Moczar's direction – thousands of students were beaten and arrested – as well as an intensified media campaign against "Zionist" elements in Poland.

forehand from a friend of mine who worked for the police.

Nevertheless, after these events my wife and I decided that I should leave right away for Denmark and that she and my daughter would remain to close down the business, joining me afterward in Copenhagen. It was to my advantage that during the anti-Jewish campaign, the government instructed the foreign passport office to provide speedy travel documents to any Jew who asked for it. After receiving the document, the applicant would have to leave Poland within two weeks.[6] Two days after receiving my papers, I was on a train to Copenhagen. Soon after my departure, several people from the so-called committee came to my studio and found only my wife. Hearing that I had left Poland, they didn't bother to conduct the audit.

A few weeks later, my wife and daughter arrived in Copenhagen. Eventually I found out that one of the conspirators took over my studio. This reminded me of events that had occurred during the German occupation. During the Nazi era, I had hidden from racist persecution. Being treated with contempt and malevolence by home-grown racists, as all Jews at that time were, became unbearable. We stayed in Copenhagen for a year, but eventually decided that it would be better for our daughter to learn English, so we made arrangements to immigrate to Canada.

We arrived in Canada in July 1970 and, like all recent immigrants, began our lives anew. Canadian Manpower and Immigration – now called Citizenship and Immigration Canada – treated us generously. They supported my family for the first five months so that we could take English-as-a-second-language courses. After that I took a course in offset printing at George Brown College for a year. It was the first

---

6 Jews who left Poland during this time were forced to renounce their Polish citizen-ship – to ensure that their departure was permanent – and to declare Israel as their destination on exit visas whether or not they were actually moving there. In this way, the Polish government acquired "proof" that the emigrants were affiliated with Israel rather than Poland.

year of a three-year course in graphic art. After I finished the first year, I started work at a printing house in the evenings while I completed the second and third year of the program. When I graduated, I was properly trained and felt competent to work in modern offset colour printing. I worked in several printing establishments until finding a satisfactory workplace at an advertising and publishing company that was a subsidiary of the TorStar corporation, where I continued to work for many years until my retirement.

Epilogue: Poland Revisited

At the beginning of my story, I mentioned that for half a century I didn't want to relive my memories of the years of the German occupation. Neither did I intend to visit the places of my wartime wanderings. But thoughts and feelings change with time. While visiting Poland in 1993, I decided to go back and see some of the places and the people with whom I had lived during those years.

When I arrived in Poland, I travelled from Warsaw to Otwock. I walked the streets that were still so familiar to me and went to the end of Karczewska Street, where my junior school had been (it was now the home of a school board). I took a photograph of the building as a reminder. I hired a taxi and went to the cemetery on the outskirts of Karczew, where my mother is buried. Overturned gravestones lay on the sandy dunes. No one was looking after the cemetery, and it had started to shrink. The town of Karczew was developing quickly and new homes were being built there. One of the houses sat right on the edge of the cemetery. Looking at the cemetery, I reflected on Jewish life in Otwock, which had ceased to exist.

I returned to Warsaw and travelled by train to Siedlce and the town of Łuków, which was close to the village where I had lived from mid-October 1942 to November 1943. After fifty years, I suddenly found myself in the place where I had been at risk every day. Remembering those times, my mind was filled with vivid images. There I was, in the middle of the village, walking down the road on which I had led the cows to pasture day after day. At that time it was a dirt road, but now it had a paved surface with tall and leafy trees on both sides. I decided to visit the railway worker first. I found his son, who had inherited the farm and had become a train conductor. When I worked for his parents, he was five years old, and they called him Janek.

Unfortunately, his parents, to whom I owed so much, are no longer alive. His sister, Kasia, who was the same age as me, lived nearby and I went to visit her, too. She told me that her other brother, Adam, who as a child loved to play the harmonica, had become a musician and was quite successful in his field. Next, I went to visit Paul Siedlecki's farm, where I had stayed in the summer of 1943 and where my fate had hung on a thread. Thanks to the fact that Paul didn't find me out by checking if I was circumcised that day in the forest, I remain alive and able to write about these events.

I approached the farm, whose buildings were so familiar to me. But now they looked shabby, the wooden fence and gate broken and falling apart. When I entered the yard, I found the doors to the house open. An elderly woman appeared in the entrance, my former employer's wife. She remembered me and, as always, she was very talkative. She told me that Paul had died a long time ago from the effects of alcohol. I wasn't surprised – I remembered Paul's love of vodka. She also told me that her daughter, Tereska, lived in the same village. I went to see her and she, too, remembered me. From her I learned the real reason for her father's death – he had been arrested by the Polish Security Services on suspicion of having a gun in his possession, and in 1953 the family received an official notice that he had died in prison and was buried there. A line by writer Henryk Sienkiewicz came to my mind: "The fate of people cannot be foretold."

I became eager to continue these visits. After returning to Warsaw, I travelled for six hours by bus to the little town of Dubeczno, near Włodawa, where I had lived for a short time in 1942 with my uncle and his family. The "Argentina" section where they had lived no longer existed, but the town itself had grown larger. There were many apartment blocks, several stories high, and smaller brick houses. Where the Jewish Argentina section had been, two small wooden houses remained, but I was afraid to go near them in case I would be overcome by emotion. While in Dubeczno I went to the municipal office, where I was told they didn't have any documents about the prior Jewish population. No trace of the Jewish inhabitants remained – they had all been sent to the Sobibor death camp. Eight kilometres away, in the village of Kozaki where I began my "career" as a herdsman, only a few small houses remained and, although I tried, I could not reach them. Once, a straight road from Dubeczno had led through bushes and shrubbery, but it was no longer there. I tried, unsuccessfully, to reach the village by a circuitous route.

I also went to see Albin in the village of Ossowa. Due to his advanced age and ailing memory, he had no recollection of my working for him and mistook me for someone else. After this last attempt to retrace my wanderings over Poland, I returned to Warsaw to complete my holiday. Thus ended my pilgrimage to the places where I had lived during the German occupation.

~

In 2004, I visited my hometown once again and discovered it anew. I became acquainted with Mr. Zbigniew Nosowski, chairman of the Citizens Committee to Memorialize the Otwock and Karczew Jews. I discovered that the committee was formed in 2002 and had its start in the presbytery of Father Wojciech Lemanski, one of its founders. During my stay in Otwock, together with Mr. Nosowski and Father Lemanski, I visited the Jewish cemeteries in Karczew and Otwock. One of the tasks that the committee had had in its short history was cleaning up the town cemetery. Among the many involved in the cleaning were students from Otwock high schools.

When I was there again in May 2005, the committee had invited Jewish youth from Australia who were taking part in the March of the Living to assist the local Polish students in cleaning up the Jewish cemetery.[1] Thanks to Mr. Nosowski, I had an opportunity to meet with the students and to tell them about my experiences during the German occupation of Poland. The committee also organized discussions about the significance of the vibrant pre-war Jewish culture, to remind the present-day inhabitants of Otwock about their co-citizens who were so instrumental in building and developing the town and its health resorts. Since the inception of the committee, every year, on August 19, many Polish inhabitants of Otwock meet at the square where eight thousand Jews were herded and then taken by cattle trains to Treblinka and their deaths. In the evening, a procession with lit candles proceeds to Reymonta Street to a stone at the mass grave of the several thousand murdered Otwock Jews. There, Jews and Christians pray together. It was there that I also met Zbigniew Skoczek, editor-in-chief of the local newspaper *Linia Otwocka* (The Otwock Line).

In the spring of 2005, the *Nowa Ziemia* (New Earth) publishing company published my memoir, *Moje Drogi Dziecinstwa 1939–1945* (The Roads of My Childhood 1939–1945). The book launch was held in the Otwock Museum, whose director was Mr. Jan Tabencki, and there were several write-ups about it in the local newspaper. I was also kindly received by the mayor of Otwock, Mr. Andrzej Szacillo, and his deputy, Mr. Robert Mroczek.

In August 2005, Wież Publishing House in Warsaw published the Polish edition of *Stepchild on the Vistula*, by Simcha Simchovitch. This book describes the writer's childhood and youth and Jewish life in Otwock between the two world wars. Recently, while translating

---

1 The March of the Living brings Jewish students and young adults from around the world to Poland and Israel to learn more about the Holocaust. For more information, see the glossary.

this book into Polish, I turned my thoughts to my own childhood. Thanks to Simchovitch's lively descriptions, Otwock came to life for me again. Walking daily to school along Świderska Street, I used to pass by the open doors of the small Jewish workshops the author so vividly describes. I am very glad that this truthful description of Jewish life in Otwock before World War II is now being published and that I had the privilege to translate it.

While in Otwock, I was proud to learn that there were more than twenty people designated as "Righteous Among the Nations" among those who had lived in Otwock. Together with their family members who helped them, they comprise over forty people. These were people who had risked their lives to save Jews during the years of the Holocaust and have been honoured by the Yad Vashem Memorial in Jerusalem. One of the recipients of the medal was Mrs. Krystyna Danko, with whom I had the honour to converse. As she explained, "My family considered helping other people as an entirely natural deed."[2]

In August 2005, I received several emails from Mr. Nosowski with information about other people who had helped Jewish children during the war, often by issuing them false documents. Among these were Father Ludwik Wolski, the Otwock parish priest; the Szpakowski family; the Sisters of the Saint Elizabeth Convent, who protected a number of Jewish children; and Bronislaw Marchlewicz, Chief of the Otwock Police at that time. In September 1945 Marchlewicz received a letter from Mrs. Hanna Kaminska that thanked him for saving her niece, Marysia Osowiecka. In 2005, he was posthumously honoured with the medal of "Righteous Among The Nations of the World" upon the recommendation of Osowiecka. During the war, Marchlewicz was a member of the underground Polish Home Army (AK) under

---

2   For more information on the title of Righteous Among the Nations, see the glossary.

the pseudonym "Smialy." The Yad Vashem medal was presented to his son, Zbigniew, by the Ambassador of Israel, Mr. David Peleg, at a ceremony in the Jewish Theatre in Warsaw.

In 2009, Father Ludwik Wolski and Jadwiga and Mieczyslaw Danko, also from Otwock, were posthumously awarded the Righteous Among the Nations title and in August 2009 they were honoured by Israeli Ambassador Zvi Rav-Ner at a ceremony at the Otwock Youth Cultural Centre on 10 Poniatowskiego Street. For all those designated as Righteous Among the Nations, the ancient rabbinic text, the Talmud, states, "Whoever saves one person saves an entire world."

Glossary

Anders, Władysław (1892–1970) General in the Polish army before and during World War II and a member of the Polish government-in-exile in London after the war. A cavalry commander on the eve of World War II, Anders was taken prisoner by Soviet forces when they invaded Poland in September 1939. In June 1941, Anders was released by the Soviets to establish an armed force of exiled Poles living in the USSR to assist the Red Army in its fight against Germany. By 1942 this force, known as the Anders Army, included approximately 72,000 combatants – among them at least 4,000-5,000 Jews. In August 1942, political tensions between Soviet authorities and the Polish government-in-exile, as well as shortages of equipment and rations, led Anders to redeploy his forces to the Middle East. There he formed the Second Corps of the Polish Armed Forces. From 1943 to 1946 Anders and his men fought alongside the British forces in Italy. After the war, Anders was stripped of his citizenship by Poland's Communist regime. He remained exiled in London until his death in 1970.

antisemitism Prejudice, discrimination, persecution and/or hatred against Jewish people, institutions, culture and symbols.

Armia Krajowa (Polish) Also known as AK or the Home Army. Formed in February 1942, the Armia Krajowa was the largest Polish resistance movement in German-occupied Poland in

World War II. Although the organization has been criticized for antisemitism and some factions were even guilty of killing Jews, it is also true that the AK established a Section for Jewish Affairs in February 1942 that collected information about what was happening to Jews in Poland, centralized contacts between Polish and Jewish military organizations, and supported the Relief Council for Jews in Poland. Members of the AK also assisted the Jewish revolt during the Warsaw ghetto uprising in 1943, both outside the ghetto walls and by joining Jewish fighters inside the ghetto. Between 1942 and 1945, hundreds of Jews joined the AK.

Aryan A nineteenth-century anthropological term originally used to refer to the Indo-European family of languages and, by extension, the peoples who spoke them. It became a synonym for people of Nordic or Germanic descent in the theories that inspired Nazi racial ideology. "Aryan" was an official classification in Nazi racial laws to denote someone of pure Germanic blood, as opposed to "non-Aryans," such as Jews, part-Jews, Roma (Gypsies) and others of supposedly inferior racial stock.

bar mitzvah (Hebrew; literally: one to whom commandments apply) The ceremony that celebrates a Jewish boy's coming of age at thirteen under Jewish religious law. Traditionally, he reads a section, or portion, from the Torah and recites the prescribed blessings at public prayer, and his father then recites a blessing of thanks. A celebration usually follows the religious service.

bet midrash (Hebrew; literally: house of learning; Yiddish, beys midrash) A Jewish religious study centre.

bimah (Hebrew) The raised platform in a synagogue from which the Torah is read.

catechism A reference text and guide to the Catholic religion in a question-and-answer format to help teach the doctrine of the faith.

Central Committee of Polish Jews Also called the Jewish Committee. An organization established in 1944 and officially recognized as the highest administrative body of Polish Jewry. The Central Committee sought to reconstruct post-war Jewish life in Poland. Between 1944 and 1950 it received funds from the Polish government, as well as from the American Jewish Joint Distribution Committee, with which it financed its work to care for Jewish refugees. It set up various departments to help survivors search for their families and document their testimonies and it provided legal assistance, social services, health care and child care (by establishing orphanages); it also disseminated reports and newsletters on the state of Jewish life in Poland.

cholent (Yiddish) A traditional Jewish slow-cooked pot stew usually eaten as the main course at the festive Shabbat lunch on Saturdays after the synagogue service and on other Jewish holidays. For Jews of Eastern-European descent, the basic ingredients of *cholent* are meat, potatoes, beans and barley.

circumcision Removal of the foreskin of the penis. In Judaism, ritual circumcision is performed on the eighth day of a male infant's life in a religious ceremony known as a *brit milah* (Hebrew) or *bris* (Yiddish) to welcome him into the covenant between God and the Children of Israel.

fifth column A term first used by the Nationalists in the Spanish Civil War of 1936–1939 to refer to their supporters within the territories controlled by the Republican side. Because these people were helping the four columns of the Nationalists' army, they were deemed to be their "fifth column." Since that time the expression has been used to designate a group of people who are clandestinely collaborating with an invading enemy.

Generalgouvernement The territory in central Poland that was conquered by the Germans in September 1939 but not annexed to the Third Reich. Made up of the districts of Warsaw, Krakow, Radom and Lublin, it was deemed a special administrative area and was used as the place for the Nazis to carry out their racial plans of murdering Jews. From 1939 onward, Jews from all over German-occupied territories were transferred to this region, as were Poles who had been expelled from their homes in the annexed Polish territories further west.

ghetto A confined residential area for Jews. The term originated in Venice, Italy in 1516 with a law requiring all Jews to live on a segregated, gated island known as Ghetto Nuovo. Throughout the Middle Ages in Europe, Jews were often forcibly confined to gated Jewish neighbourhoods. During the Holocaust, the Nazis forced Jews to live in crowded and unsanitary conditions in run-down districts of cities and towns. Most ghettos in Poland were enclosed by brick walls or wooden fences with barbed wire. The Warsaw ghetto was the largest in Poland with over 400,000 Jews crowded into an area of just over 300 hectares; the Lodz ghetto was the second-largest, with over 160,000 inhabitants.

Gomułka, Władysław (1905–1982) First Secretary of the Polish Worker's Party (1956–1970). At first, he promised economic reforms and liberalization under Communist rule. However, his reforms (known as Gomułka's thaws, Polish October or October 1956) were temporary, and soon came under Soviet criticism. Gomułka followed Soviet policy thereafter, which was specifically anti-Israel after the Soviet Union sided with the Arab nations (Jordan, Syria, Egypt) after the Six-Day War. He specifically initiated propaganda and rhetoric aimed at Jews in his infamous June 1967 speech, targeting Zionists and equating Jews with Zionism, thus beginning a new wave of antisemitism in Poland, which eventually resulted in the emigration of over 25,000 Jews from Poland. *See also* Six-Day War.

Hashomer Hatzair (Hebrew) The Youth Guard. Hashomer Hatzair, a left-wing Zionist youth movement, was founded in Central Europe in the early twentieth century to prepare young Jews to become workers and farmers who would establish kibbutzim – collective settlements – in pre-state Israel and work the land as pioneers. Before World War II, there were 70,000 Hashomer

Hatzair members worldwide and many of those in Nazi-occupied territories led resistance activities in the ghettos and the concentration camps or joined partisan groups in the forests of east-central Europe. It is the oldest Zionist youth movement still in existence.

Hasidism (from the Hebrew word *hasid*; literally: piety) A Jewish spiritual movement founded by Rabbi Israel ben Eliezer in eighteenth-century Poland; characterized by philosophies of mysticism and focusing on joyful prayer. It stressed piety and joyful worship over the intellectual study of the Talmud. This resulted in a new kind of *rebbe* or leader who attracted disciples as opposed to the traditional rabbis who focused on the intellectual study of Jewish law. Melody and dance play an important role in Hasidic worship.

Jewish burial society (Aramaic; *chevra kadisha*, literally "holy society") An organization comprised of Jewish volunteers that helps prepare the body for burial according to Jewish ritual and law.

Jewish ghetto police (in German, Ordnungsdienst; literally: "Order Service") The Jewish ghetto police force was established by the Jewish Councils on the orders of the Germans. The force, who were armed with clubs, was created to carry out various tasks in the ghettos, such as traffic control and guarding the ghetto gates. Eventually, some policemen also participated in rounding up Jews for forced labour and transportation to the death camps. There has been much debate and controversy surrounding the role of the Jewish Councils and the Jewish police. But even though the Jewish police exercised considerable power within the ghetto, to the Germans these policemen were "just" Jews and subject to the same fate as other Jews.

Judenrat (German; plural: *Judenräte*) Jewish Council. A group of Jewish leaders appointed by the Germans to administer and provide services to the local Jewish population under occupation and carry out German orders. The *Judenräte* appeared to be self-governing entities, but were under complete German control. The *Judenräte* faced difficult and complex moral decisions under brutal conditions and remain a contentious subject. The chairmen had to decide whether to comply or refuse to comply with German demands. Some were killed by the Nazis for refusing, while others committed suicide. Jewish officials who advocated compliance thought that cooperation might save at least some Jews. Some who denounced resistance efforts did so because they believed that armed resistance would bring death to the entire community.

judenrein (German; literally: free or cleansed of Jews). A pejorative term used by the Nazis to describe an area from which all the Jews had been removed, *judenrein* deliberately carried connotations of cleanliness and purity, maliciously suggesting that the presence of Jews defiled a location.

kibbutz (Hebrew) A collectively owned farm or settlement in Israel democratically governed by its members.

Kielce pogrom In the city of Kielce, where about 250 Jews lived after the war (the pre-war Jewish population had been over 20,000), riots broke out in July 1946 after the false account of a young Polish boy kidnapped by Jews emerged. In retaliation, police arrested and beat Jewish residents, which incited a mob of hundreds of Polish civilians, who violently attacked and killed forty Jews while police stood by. This event, combined with other antisemitic incidents throughout Poland (other pogroms occurred in Rzeszów, Krakow, Tarnów and Sosnowiec, and robberies and blackmail were common) was the catalyst for a mass exodus of Jews from Poland – between July 1945 and September 1946, more than 80,000 Jews left Poland.

Lord's Prayer The New Testament "Lord's Prayer," also known as the "Our Father," is the best-known prayer in Christianity.

March of the Living Established in 1988, this annual event takes place in April on Holocaust Memorial Day (Yom HaShoah) in Poland

and aims to educate primarily Jewish students and young adults from around the world about the Holocaust and Jewish life during World War II. Along with Holocaust survivors, participants march the three kilometres from Auschwitz to Birkenau to commemorate all who perished in the Holocaust. The concept of the March of the Living comes from the Nazi death marches that Jews were forced to go on when they were being evacuated from the forced labour and concentration camps at the very end of the war. Many Jews died during these marches, and thus the March of the Living was created to both remember and contrast this history, by celebrating Jewish life and strength. After spending time in Poland, participants travel to Israel and join in celebrations there for Israel's remembrance and independence days.

Mazur A Polish dialect generally spoken in the central and eastern regions of Poland.

minyan (Hebrew) The quorum of ten adult male Jews required for certain religious rites. The term can also designate a congregation.

Mourner's Kaddish Also known as the Mourner's Prayer, Kaddish is said as part of mourning rituals in Jewish prayer services as well as at funerals and memorials. Sons are required to say Kaddish daily for eleven months after the death of a parent and also each year, on the anniversary of the death. The word Kaddish comes from the Hebrew root "holy."

partisans Members of irregular military forces or resistance movements formed to oppose armies of occupation. During World War II there were a number of different partisan groups that opposed both the Nazis and their collaborators in several countries. The term partisan could include highly organized, almost paramilitary groups such as the Red Army partisans; ad hoc groups bent more on survival than resistance; and roving groups of bandits who plundered what they could from all sides during the war. There were members of Polish resistance groups who hid out in forests and depended on the cooperation of farmers for food and shelter. There were several Polish resistance movements, often fiercely opposed to one another on ideological grounds, and at least one, the National Armed Forces, was violently antisemitic.

Piłsudski, Józef (1867–1935) Leader of the Second Polish Republic from 1926 to 1935. Piłsudski is considered to be a hero and is largely responsible for achieving Poland's independence in 1918 after more than a century of being partitioned by Russia, Austria and Prussia. Piłsudski's regime was notable for the improvement in the situation of ethnic minorities, including Poland's large Jewish population. He followed a policy of "state-assimilation" whereby citizens were judged not by their ethnicity but by their loyalty to the state. Many Polish Jews felt that his regime was key in keeping the antisemitic currents in Poland in check; many voted for him and actively participated in his political bloc. When he died in 1935, the quality of life of Poland's Jews deteriorated once again. Until his death, he also managed to keep both Hitler and Stalin at bay, resisting Germany's attempts to pressure Poland into an alliance against the USSR and extending a Soviet-Polish nonaggression treaty to 1945.

Polish recovered territories Also known as the Western and Northern territories, these areas encompassed previously German areas in Western Pomerania, Lubusz Land, Silesia, Gdańsk and Warmia and Masuria. The territories were ceded to Poland in 1945 as part of the post-war redrawing of borders. Polish and Ukrainian civilians were encouraged to live in these areas, from which most of the ethnic German population had been expelled. The city of Wrocław, for example, was ceded to Poland and the German population of the city was officially transferred to Germany. It was replaced with a Polish population from the former Polish city Lvov, which in turn was ceded to the Soviet Union.

rebbe (Yiddish; teacher) The spiritual leader or teacher of a Hasidic movement. *See also* Hasidism.

Righteous Among the Nations A title bestowed by Yad Vashem, the Holocaust Martyrs' and Heroes' Remembrance Authority, to honour non-Jews who risked their lives to help save Jews during the Holocaust. A commission was established in 1963 to award the title. After a name is submitted and fits certain criteria and their story is carefully corroborated, honourees are awarded with a medal and certificate and are commemorated on the Wall of Honour at the Garden of the Righteous in Jerusalem.

Rokossovsky, Konstantin (1896–1968) Soviet marshal and commander of the Red Army forces liberating Poland in 1944, and specifically Warsaw. Following Stalin's orders, his forces denied support to the independent Polish Home Army uprising against the German occupation in Warsaw in 1944. The initiators of the uprising hoped to create an independent Poland, while the Soviet Union insisted on a Soviet-allied state. Rokossovsky and his army did not enter and liberate Warsaw until January 1945.

Sabbath/ Shabbat (Hebrew; in Yiddish, Shabbes, Shabbos) The weekly day of rest beginning Friday at sunset and ending Saturday at sundown ushered in by the lighting of candles on Friday night and the recitation of blessings over wine and challah (egg bread); a day of celebration as well as prayer, it is customary to eat three festive meals, attend synagogue services and refrain from doing any work or travelling.

SD Abbreviation for Sicherheitsdienst, the security and intelligence service of the SS. The main responsibility of the SD, which was headed by Reinhard Heydrich under the command of Heinrich Himmler, was to seek out supposed enemies of the Third Reich through huge networks of informants in the occupied territories.

shtetl (Yiddish) Small town. A small village or town with a predominantly Jewish population that existed before World War II in Central and Eastern Europe, where life revolved around Judaism and Judaic culture. In the Middle Ages, Jews were not allowed to own land, and so the shtetl developed as a refuge for Jews.

Six-Day War The armed conflict between Israel and the neighbouring states of Egypt, Jordan, and Syria that took place from June 5–10,

1967. In response to Egypt closing the Straits of Tiran to Israeli shipping, the creation of an alliance between Egypt, Syria and Jordan, and the mobilization of troops by Egypt's leader Gamal Nasser along Israel's borders, Israel launched a pre-emptive attack. In the days that followed, Israeli forces drove the armies back and occupied the Sinai Peninsula, Gaza Strip, West Bank and Golan Heights. Israel also reunited Jerusalem, the eastern half of which Jordan had controlled since the 1948–1949 war.

Sobibor A death camp located in the Lublin district of the *Generalgouvernement*, Sobibor was the second camp built under Operation Reinhard – the German code word for the Nazi plan for the mass extermination of European Jews. The camp was built between October 1941 and April 1942, and began gassing operations in May of that year. Jews were deported to Sobibor from ghettos in the northern and eastern regions of the Lublin district, from German-occupied Soviet territory, and from Germany, Austria, Slovakia, Bohemia and Moravia, Netherlands and France. More than 150,000 prisoners were killed there. On October 14, 1943, the prisoners staged an uprising, and three hundred of the six hundred inmates escaped, although many were later found and shot.

soltys (Polish) Chairman of a village council.

SS Abbreviation for Schutzstaffel (Defence Corps). The SS was established in 1925 as Adolf Hitler's elite corps of personal bodyguards. Under the directorship of its leader, Heinrich Himmler, its membership grew from 280 in 1929 to 50,000 when the Nazis came to power in 1933 and nearly a quarter of a million on the eve of World War II. The SS was comprised of the Allgemeine-SS (General SS) and the Waffen-SS (Armed, or Combat SS). The General SS dealt with policing and the enforcement of Nazi racial policies in Germany and the Nazi-occupied countries. An important unit within the SS was the Reichssicherheitshauptamt (RSHA, the Central Office of Reich Security), whose responsibility included the Gestapo (Geheime Staatspolizei). The SS ran the concentration and death camps, with all their associated econom-ic enterprises, and also fielded its own Waffen-SS military divi-sions, including some recruited from the occupied countries.

Star of David (in Hebrew, *Magen David*) The six-pointed star that is the ancient and most recognizable symbol of Judaism. During World War II, Jews in Nazi-occupied areas were frequently forced to wear a badge or armband with the Star of David on it as an identifying mark of their lesser status and to single them out as targets for persecution.

synagogue (in Yiddish, shul) A Jewish house of prayer.

Szmalcownik The term used for people who either blackmailed Jews or denounced them to the Gestapo.

tallit (in Yiddish, *tallis*) Four-cornered ritual garment traditionally worn by adult Jewish men during the morning prayer and on the Day of Atonement (Yom Kippur). One usually wears the *tallit* over one's shoulders but some choose to place it over their heads to express awe in the presence of God.

Talmud (Hebrew; literally: "instruction" or "learning") The Talmud is an ancient rabbinic text that discusses and debates Jewish his-tory, law and ethics; it is comprised of two sections: the Mishnah, which is further subdivided into six sections and focuses on legal issues, and the Gemara, which analyzes the legal issues.

Torah (Hebrew) The Five Books of Moses (the first five books in the Bible), also called the Pentateuch. The Torah is the core of Jewish scripture, traditionally believed to have been given to Moses on Mount Sinai. In Christianity it is referred to as the "Old Testament."

Treblinka A labour and death camp created as part of Operation Reinhard, the German code word for the Nazi plan for the mass ex-termination of European Jews. A slave-labour camp (Treblinka I) was built in November 1941 in the *Generalgouvernement*, near the villages of Treblinka and Makinia Górna, about 80 kilometres northeast of Warsaw in Poland. Treblinka II, the killing centre, was constructed in a sparsely populated and heavily wooded area about 1.5 kilometres from the labour camp. The first massive deportations to Treblinka II from Warsaw began on July 22, 1942. The people who arrived packed into railway freight cars were separated by sex, stripped of their clothing and other possessions, marched into buildings that they were told contained bathhouses and gassed with carbon monoxide. From July 1942 to October 1943 more than 750,000 Jews were killed at Treblinka, making it second only to Auschwitz in the numbers of Jews killed. Treblinka I and II were both liberated by the Soviet army in July 1944.

Ukrainian Greek Catholic Church Also known as the Ukrainian Catholic Church. The church follows the Pope and the Eastern rites; in post-war Communist Poland, the church officially became the Russian Orthodox Church.

Ukrainische Hilfspolizei (German) Ukrainian Auxiliary Police. The Ukrainian Auxiliary Police was formed in the wake of the German occupation of eastern Poland and the Ukraine in June 1941 and actively collaborated with the Nazis in the implementation of their plans to persecute and eventually mass murder Jews. The Ukrainian Auxiliary Police escorted Jews to forced labour sites, guarded the ghettos and engaged in mass-murder shooting operations.

Virgin Mary Prayer The Hail Mary prayer, also knows as the Angelic Salutation or Ave Maria, is both a common Catholic prayer and a significant element of the Rosary, a traditional devotional prayer.

Volksdeutsche The term used for ethnic Germans who lived outside Germany in Central and Eastern Europe; also refers to the ethnic German colonists who were resettled in Polish villages as part of far-reaching Nazi plans to Germanize Nazi-occupied territories in the East.

Wächter, Otto (1901–1949) Governor of Krakow in the Nazi *Generalgouvernement*. He was a member of the SA and then the

SS and played a leading role in organizing the mass murder of the Jews of Poland.

Warsaw Ghetto Uprising The largest single revolt by Jews during the Holocaust, the Warsaw Ghetto Uprising developed in response to the Nazis' deportation of more than 275,000 ghetto inhabitants to slave-labour and death camps and the murder of another 10,000 of them between July and September 1942. When the Germans initiated the liquidation of the ghetto's remaining population of approximately 60,000 Jews by deporting them to the Treblinka death camp on April 19, 1943, about 750 organized ghetto fighters launched an insurrection. Despite some support from Jewish and Polish resistance organizations outside the ghetto, the poorly armed insurgents were crushed by the Germans after a month on May 16, 1943. More than 56,000 Jews were captured; about 7,000 were shot and the remainder were deported to death camps and concentration camps.

Warsaw uprising An uprising organized by the Polish Home Army (AK) to liberate Warsaw from German occupation and initiate the establishment of an independent Poland in the post-war period. In August 1944, as the Soviet Red Army neared Praga, a suburb of Warsaw situated on the east bank of the Vistula River, the uprising began. The AK, however, had only 2,500 weapons for its 40,000 troops and the Soviets, under Joseph Stalin's orders, did not give support to the uprising. By October 2, 1944, the attempt at liberation had been crushed and the results were devastating – more than 150,000 civilians had been killed, and more than 25 per cent of Warsaw had been destroyed.

White Russians Also known as "white émigrés." White Russians is an outdated term used to denote Russians who fought against the Soviet Red Army and Bolshevism during the 1917–1920 Russian civil war.

wójt (Polish) The elected mayor of a rural municipality, or commune, in Poland made up of small villages.

Yad Vashem The Holocaust Martyrs' and Heroes' Remembrance Authority established in 1953 to commemorate, educate the public about, research and document the Holocaust.

Yiddish A language derived from Middle High German with elements of Hebrew, Aramaic, Romance and Slavic languages, and written in Hebrew characters. There are similarities between Yiddish and contemporary German.

Zionism A movement promoted by the Viennese Jewish journalist Theodor Herzl, who argued in his 1896 book *Der Judenstaat* (The Jewish State) that the best way to resolve the problem of antisemitism and persecution of Jews in Europe was to create an independent Jewish state in the historic Jewish homeland of Biblical Israel. Zionists promoted the revival of Hebrew as a Jewish national language. In interwar Poland, Zionism was one of many Jewish political parties with affiliated schools and youth groups.

Appendices

Der Distriktschef von Krakau

ANORDNUNG
Kennzeichnung der Juden im Distrikt Krakau

Ich ordne an, dass alle Juden im Alter von über 12 Jahren im Distrikt Krakau mit Wirkung vom 1. 12. 1939 ausserhalb ihrer eigenen Wohnung ein sichtbares Kennzeichen zu tragen haben. Dieser Anordnung unterliegen auch nur vorübergehend im Distriktsbereich anwesende Juden für die Dauer ihres Aufenthaltes.

Als Jude im Sinne dieser Anordnung gilt:

1. wer der mosaischen Glaubensgemeinschaft angehört oder angehört hat,
2. jeder, dessen Vater oder Mutter der mosaischen Glaubensgemeinschaft angehört oder angehört hat.

Als Kennzeichen ist am rechten Oberarm der Kleidung und der Überkleidung eine Armbinde zu tragen, die auf weissem Grunde an der Aussenseite einen blauen Zionstern zeigt. Der weisse Grund muss eine Breite von mindestens 10 cm. haben, der Zionstern muss so gross sein, dass dessen gegenüberliegende Spitzen mindestens 8 cm. entfernt sind. Der Balken muss 1 cm. breit sein.

Juden, die dieser Verpflichtung nicht nachkommen, haben strenge Bestrafung zu gewärtigen.

Für die Ausführung dieser Anordnung. Insbesondere die Versorgung der Juden mit Kennzeichen, sind die Ältestenräte verantwortlich.

Krakau, den 18. 11. 1939.

gez. *Wächter*
Gouverneur

Szef dystryktu krakowskiego

ROZPORZĄDZENIE
Znamionowanie żydów w okręgu Krakowa

Zarządzam z ważnością od dnia 1. XII. 1939, iż wszyscy żydzi w wieku ponad 12 lat winni nosić widoczne znamiona. Rozporządzeniu temu podlegają także na czas ich pobytu przejściowo w obrębie okręgu przebywający żydzi.

Żydem w myśl tego rozporządzenia jest:

1) ten, który jest lub był wyznania mojżeszowego,
2) każdy, którego ojciec, lub matka są lub byli wyznania mojżeszowego.

Znamieniem jest biała przepaska noszona na prawym rękawie ubrania lub odzienia wierzchniego z niebieską gwiazdą sjonistyczną. Przepaska winna mieć szerokość conajmniej 10 cm, a gwiazda średnicę 8 cm. Wstążka, z której sporządzono gwiazdę, winna mieć szerokość conajmniej 1 cm.

Niestosujący się do tego zarządzenia zostaną surowo ukarani.

Za wykonanie niniejszego zarządzenia, zwłaszcza za dostarczenie opasek czynią odpowiedzialną Radę starszych.

Kraków, dnia 18. XI. 1939.

(–) *Wächter*
Gubernator

THE CHIEF OF THE DISTRICT OF KRAKOW

OFFICIAL ORDER

IDENTIFYING MARKS FOR JEWS IN THE KRAKOW DISTRICT

I herewith order that all the Jews who are twelve years old and older are required to wear a visible sign outside of their own apartment in the district of Krakow beginning December 1, 1939. This order also applies to Jews who find themselves only temporarily in the territory of the District, for the whole time of their stay.

For the purposes of this order, a Jew is:
   1 a person who is or was of the Mosaic religion;
   2 or, whose father or mother is or was of the Mosaic religion.

The sign is a white band with a blue Star of David, to be worn on the right sleeve of any garment. The band must be at least 10 cm wide, and the star must be 8 cm in diameter. The branches of the star should be at least 1 cm wide.

Violators of this order will be severely punished.

The Committee of Elders is responsible for the implementation of this regulation, and especially for providing the bands.

Krakow, November 18, 1939
Wächter
Governor [of Krakow]

Dystrykt Warszawski

Kreishauptmann
Powiatu Warszawskiego

Warszawa, 4 listopada 1940 r.

Obwieszczenie

Dotyczy żydowskiej dzielnicy mieszkaniowej:

1) W Otwocku należy utworzyć osobną „żydowską dzielnicę mieszkaniową".

Dzielnica ta ma następujące granice: Em. Plater z wyłączeniem (od granicy miasta do ul. Samorządowej) ul. Samorządowa z wyłączeniem (od ul. Em. Plater do Czaplickiego), ul. Czaplickiego (od ul. Samorządowej do ul. Warszawskiej) ul. Warszawska obustronnie (od ul. Czaplickiego do granicy miasta), granica miasta od ul. Warszawskiej do ul. Em. Plater, przejście dla pieszych przez tor [vis a vis ul. Samorządowej], granica terenów kolejowych od przejścia dla pieszych do ulicy Orlej z wyłączeniem, ul. Karczewska z wyłączeniem do ul. Olszowej bez nazwy, między ul. Bazarową i Kolejową, ul. Staszica obustronnie do toru kolejki, tor kolejki od Staszica do ul. Olszowej ul. Olszowa od toru kolejki do ul. Letniej strona północna (jednostronnie), ul. Letnia strona północna (jednostronnie od ul. Olszowej do Szkolnej, ul. bez nazwy strona północna (jednostronnie) od ul. Szkolnej do ul. Wiejskiej, ul. Wiejska wschodnia strona (jednostronnie) od ul. Olszowej do ul. Wiejskiej, granica miasta od ul. Wiejskiej, granica miasta od toru kolejki do toru kolejowego, granice terenów kolejowych od granicy miasta do przejścia dla pieszych.

2) Następnie należy utworzyć cztery „żydowskie dzielnice kuracyjne" w następujących granicach: Granica północna pomiędzy posiadłością szpitala „Zofiówka" od ul. Kochanowskiego do granicy terenu „Brijus", granica północna posiadł terenu „Brijus" granicą terenu „Brijus" i terenu sanatorium, Warszawy do ul. Wjazd do „Brijus", od ul. Wjazd do „Brijus" granicą prywatnych posesji do ul. Kochanowskiego wejęcie z posesją Szpitala) ul. Kochanowskiego (strona zachodnia) do ul. Świerkowej, ul. Świerkowa obustronnie od ul. Kochanowskiego do ul. Żeromskiego, ul. Żeromskiego z wyłączeniem (od ul. Świerkowej do Wierzbowej) ul. Wierzbowa obustronnie, od ul. Żeromskiego do ul. Kochanowskiego, ul. Kochanowskiego do ul. Wierzbowej-granica „Zofiówka".

3) Termin wymaganego przesiedlenia ustala się na dzień 1.12.1940. Po tym terminie zarówno w żydowskiej dzielnicy mieszkaniowej jak i w żydowskiej dzielnicy kuracyjnej mogą zamieszkiwać TYLKO ŻYDZI. Niemcy i Polacy winni ulokować się w innych częściach miasta.

Należy również natychmiast rozpocząć przesunięcie znajdujących się w żydowskich dzielnicach mieszkaniowej i kuracyjnej polskich przedsiębiorstw i sklepów.

Ostateczny termin zlikwidowania polskich przedsiębiorstw jest 1.2. 1941.

Do dnia 1.12.1940 mogą Żydzi zabrać ze sobą swoje urządzenie do nowych mieszkań. Po tym terminie jest to wzbronione.

4) Pobyt w żydowskiej dzielnicy kuracyjnej jest dozwolony tylko za pozwoleniem wydanym tylko w pilnowanym zezwoleniem lekarza miejskiego.

5) Mieszkania, które w trzech przesiedlenia będą zwolnione przez żydów i zajmowane przez polaków, winny być przed wprowadzeniem się do nich polaków gruntownie oczyszczone i zdezynfekowane przez Żydów tak na ich koszt. Należ nad tym sprawować lekarz miejski.

6) Żydzi zaś mogą prawo od godziny 19-ej wieczorem do godziny 8-ej rano przebywać poza obrębem swojej dzielnicy mieszkaniowej, nie wolno im również dzielnicę to opuszczać od soboty od godz. 19-ej do poniedziałku do godz. 6 rano.

7) Zwolnione domy żydowskie winny być aż do odwołania zarządzane przez ustanowionego przez burmistrza administratora, który w tym charakterze występuje jako pracownik Zarządu Miejskiego. Osiągnięte dochody, o ile nie zostaną zużyte na utrzymanie domu, na pokrycie danin publicznych i na wynagrodzenie administratora, należy wpłacić do Kasy Miejskiej i trzymać do dyspozycji p. Stała Dystrykt(Wydział Treuhandauszenstelle) lub do dyspozycji Kreishauptmanna.

8) Burmistrz i Rada żydowska odpowiedzialni są za przeprowadzenie wymienionego przesiedlenia i wykonanie niniejszych w związku z tym zarządzeń. Burmistrz jest upoważniony przy przeprowadzaniu niniejszych zarządzeń posługiwać się pomocą policji polskiej.

9) Przykroczenie byłe z niniejszem z innemi niniejszego zarządzeniami przeprowadzenia do żydowskiej dzielnicy mieszkaniowej przesiąga po dniu 1.12. 1940 nadal zakazane. Wygłis są dopuszczalne tylko za pisemnem zezwoleniem Kreishauptmanna.

(podp.) **Dr. Rupprecht**

Druk. W. Rączanowski, Otwock

Warsaw, November 4, 1940

The Kreishauptmann[1]
District of Warsaw

ANNOUNCEMENT

Re: Jewish Residential Quarter

The establishment of the "Jewish Residential Quarter" in Otwock has been initiated.

1 The borders of this district shall be: [here follows a list of streets and sections of streets].
2 Subsequently, a separate "Jewish Health Resort Area" shall be established within the following borders: [here follows a list of streets and sections of streets].
3 The resettlement of the Jews must be completed by December 1, 1940. After this date ONLY JEWS are allowed to reside within the Jewish Health Resort and Residential Quarter. Germans and Poles must relocate to other sections of the city.

    Polish stores and businesses should begin moving out of the Jewish Health Resort and Residential Quarter immediately. **As of January 1, 1941, all Polish establishments must be evacuated.**

    Up until December 1, 1940, Jews may take their belongings to their new living quarters; after this date they will be forbidden to do so.

    Only those [Poles] with written permission from the city's medical officer are permitted to reside in the Jewish Health Resort Area.

---

1 Sub-district Commander

4 Residences vacated by Jews during the resettlement to be occupied by Poles are to be thoroughly cleaned and disinfected before Polish residents move into them. This shall be done by the Jews themselves or at cost and supervised by the city's medical officer.

5 All Jews are forbidden to be outside their areas of residence on weekdays between 7 p.m. and 8 a.m. and from Saturday 7 p.m. until Monday 8 a.m.

6 Until further notice, vacated Jewish property shall be managed by an administrator appointed by the Mayor, who will work on behalf of the Municipal Council. Any income obtained from the properties, if not spent on maintenance, payment of public levies, or for the salary of the administrator, shall be paid into the City Fund and kept at the disposal of the Chief of the District (the Treuhandaussenstelle Department) or the Kreishauptmann.

7 The Mayor and the Jewish Council are responsible for the above resettlement to the new quarters.

8 The Mayor of the town, while performing these duties, may use the assistance of the Polish Police.

9 As of December 1, 1940, Jews from other locations are forbidden to enter the Jewish quarter. Exceptions are allowed only with a written permit from the Kreishauptmann.

(Sub-district Lieutenant) *Dr. Rupprecht*

b. pilne- terminowe

BURMISTRZ
MIASTA OTWOCKA

Otwock, dnia 19 listopada 1940.

N.I-12.

D o

Kierownika Komisariatu Policji Polskiej

w O t w o c k u

p.B. Marchlewicza

/do rąk własnych/

Na skutek decyzji Pana Kreishauptmanna niżej wymienione nieruchomości zostały włączone do "żydowskich dzielnic mieszkaniowej i kuracyjnej", wobec czego proszę Pana o niezwłoczne powiadomienie wszystkich zamieszkałych w tych nieruchomościach polaków, że, stosownie do zarządzenia p.Kreishauptmanna, winni w terminie nieprzekraczalnym do dnia 1 grudnia r.b. opuścić te domy i przenieść się do dzielnicy chrześciańskiej/polskiej./

Należy ich ostrzec, że niewykonanie tego zarządzenia w oznaczonym terminie może spowodować b.poważne konsekwencje.

Należy również pouczyć dozorców tych domów, że tylko oni mogą pozostać do dnia 1 stycznia 1941 r., by dać im możność w oznaczonym terminie urządzić swoje interesy i przenieść się na mieszkanie poza dzielnicę żydowską.

BURMISTRZ

Jan Brzdowski

Otrzymują odpisy do wiadomości:

1 / Policja Kryminalna
2 / Rada Żydowska

VERY URGENT

Otwock, the 19 of November 1940

To: the Chief of the Polish Police Station
Otwock
Mr. Bronislaw Marchlewicz
(*to be handed over personally*)

Subsequent to the decision of the Kreishauptmann[Warsaw District],
the properties mentioned below will be incorporated into the Jewish
Residential Quarter. I therefore ask you to <u>immediately</u> inform all
Polish occupants that in accordance with the order of Kreishauptmann they must vacate these properties no later than <u>December</u> 1
of this year and move into the Christian/Polish Residential Quarter.
They must be warned that failing to obey this order within the prescribed time will result in very serious consequences.
Caretakers should also be instructed that they alone may stay <u>until</u>
<u>January 1, 1941</u> in order to enable them to settle their affairs and move
outside the Jewish Residential Quarter within the prescribed time.

Mayor
Jan Gadomski

The following parties will be receiving copies for their records:
1) Criminal Police
2) Jewish Council

O B W I E S Z C Z E N I E

W związku z zarządzeniem p. Kreishauptmanna, podaję do
wiadomości co następuje:

1. Decyzja p.Kreishauptmanna co do ustalenia "żydowskich dzielnic mieszkaniowych i kuracyjnych" jest ostateczna i nie u-
   legnie żadnym zmianom, dlatego też wszelkie prośby o zmia-
   nie granic są bezcelowe i uwzględniane nie będą.

2. Wyznaczony przez p. Kreishauptmanna termin przesiedlenia się
   polaków "z dzielnic żydowskich", a żydów do dzielnic żydowskich do dnia 1 grudnia r.b. jest ostateczny.
   Niewykonanie w terminie tego zarządzenia spowoduje bardzo po-
   ważne konsekwencje.

3. Celem ścisłego i terminowego wykonania powyższego zarządzenia,
   należy nie odkładać na ostatnie dnie zamianę mieszkań wzgl.
   wynajmowanie takowych.

Otwock, dnia 20.XI.1940.　　　　　　　　BURMISTRZ

　　　　　　　　　　　　　　　　　　Jan Gadomski

Stwierdzam zgodność poryższej kserokopii z
oryginałem przechowywanym w tut. Archiwum w
zespole "Akta miasta Otwocka 1916-49 "sygn. 1057

1991. 11. 15

ANNOUNCEMENT

In accordance with the orders of the Kreishauptmann, please be informed of the following:

1 The decision of the Kreishauptmann to establish the "Jewish Health Resort and Residential Quarter" is final, with no possibility of any changes. Any request regarding a modification to the borders is therefore to no avail.
2 The fixed date set by the Kreishauptmann to resettle Poles from the Jewish quarter and to move Jews into the Jewish quarter is December 1, 1940. This date is definite and final. Failure to follow these orders in time will lead to very serious consequences.
3 To make sure that the above orders are carried out precisely and promptly, do not leave this to the last day.

Otwock, November 20, 1940.
MAYOR
[signed]

Jan Gadomski

Rada Żydowska m. Otwocka

L.1827/40.

G

Do

Pana Burmistrza

m.Otwocka

    Zgodnie z pismem Pana Burmistrza z dn.29.XI.1940r.
Nr.I-12, Rada Żydowska m.Otwocka ma zaszczyt podać do wiadomości Pana Burmistrza, że przesiedlenie żydowskich mie-
szkańców m.Otwocka do żydowskich dzielnic /mieszkaniowej
i kuracyjnej/ ukończone zostało z dniem 30 listopada 1940r.

                   Przewodniczący Rady Żydowskiej
                         m.Otwocka

Otwock,dnia 4 grudnia 1940r.

From: The Jewish Council of Otwock

TO: THE MAYOR OF THE TOWN OF OTWOCK

Pursuant to the correspondence sent by Mr. Mayor, dated November 29, 1940, #1–12, the Jewish Council of Otwock respectfully informs the Mayor that the relocation of the Jewish inhabitants in Otwock to the established Jewish quarter has been completed as of November 30, 1940.

Chairman of the Jewish Council,

[signed]

Otwock, December 4, 1940

Dotyczy: dzielnic żydowskich.

1.) Na rozkaz Gubernatora ogłasza się wszystkie dzielnice żydowskie jako zamknięte ghetta. Przeto od tej chwili zabrania się żydom opuszczać swoje dzielnice zamieszkania. W miejscowościach,w których nie zostały urządzone specjalne dzielnice żydowskie,a w których żydzi mieszkają tylko w oddzielnych domach,nie wolno żydom tej miejscowości opuścić.

2.) Wejścia do dzielnic żydowskich należy zamknąć przez stawienie drewnianych lub drucianych płotów,zostawiając tylko dostęp dla policji,straży pożarnej i transportów pierwszej potrzeby.

3.) Do opuszczania ghetta upoważnieni są tylko ci żydzi, którzy.posiadają przepustkę wystawioną przez Kreishauptmanna,. przez właściwy posterunek żandamerii,przez niemieckiego urzędnika komisariatu policji kryminalnej lub przez niemieckiego urzędnika właściwego Oddziału Urzędu Pracy. Tak samo mogą opuszczać ghetto drużyny robotnicze pod eskortą policji.

4.) Niemcom i Polakom jest wstęp do ghetta wzbroniony. Do wejścia na teren ghetta upoważniony jest jedynie Kreishauptmann lub jego zastępca,lekarz powiatowy lub jego zastępca, niemiecka i polska policja włącznie Policji Kryminalnej,kierownik właściwego Oddziału Urzędu Pracy,burmistrz lub wójt danej miejscowości i te osoby,które posiadają przepustkę wystawioną przez Kreishauptmanna lub jeden z urzędów niemieckich wymienionych pod ad 3.).

5.) Za przepustkę upoważniającą do opuszczenia wzgl. do wstępu na teren ghetta mogą być pobierane opłaty w wysokości od zł.5,- do zł.50c, ,które wpłyną po potrąca do Kasy Kreishauptmanna i do kasy gminnej.

6.) Na ulicach dojazdowych ghetta,należy umieścić tablica z następującym napisem: "Jüdisches Wohngebiet.Betreten durch Deutsche und Polen verboten. Dzielnica żydowska.Niemcom i Polakom wstęp wzbroniony. Der Kreishauptmann".

7.) Wykroczenia przeciwko niniejszemu zarządzeniu karane będą grzywną do zł. 1.000,- lub robotami przymusowymi lub aresztem. W razie niemożności zapłacenia przez żyd.sprawcę odpowiada za pokrycie grzywny Rada Żydowska. Wykraczających przeciwko zarządzeniu należy zaaresztować. Należy składać doniesienia.

8.) O zamknięciu ulic dojazdowych i ustawieniu tablic z nakazem należy mi zakomunikować do 5.2.41 r.

9.) Odpis niniejszego zarządzenia należy dostarczyć właściwej Radzie Żydowskiej za pokwitowaniem odbioru.

Stwierdzam zgodność niniejszej księgokopii z oryginałem przechowywanym w tut. Archiwum I respole, Akta miasta Chm... 1916-49 " sygn. 1063

lo.) Wszystkim burmistrzom i wójtom nakłada się
obowiązek ostrego zastosowania wymienionych środków w
çelu zapobieżenia swobodnego przenoszenia się żydów.

/-/ Dr.Rupprecht

Odpis:

żandameria niemiecka
komisariat pol.krym.w Otwocku,Pruszkowie i Wołominie
pclicja polska.

Organe pclicji są odpowiedzialne ze przestrzega-
nie przez żydów zakazu opuszczania ghetta i miejsca zamieszkania;przeciwko wykraczającym należy postępować
bezwzględnie zastosowując wyżej wymienione środki.

RE: THE JEWISH RESIDENTIAL QUARTER

1 In accordance with the order of the Governor, all Jewish quarters are henceforth declared closed ghettos. From this date on, it is prohibited for all Jews to leave their areas of residence. In locations where special Jewish quarters have not been established but separate houses have been assigned to Jews, it is prohibited for Jews to leave their places of dwelling.

2 Entry into the Jewish Residential Area is to be blocked by erecting wooden or wire fences, leaving access only for the police, fire department, and emergency transportation.

3 Only those Jews who have passes issued by the Kreishauptmann, authorized police, a German civil servant, the criminal police, or the designated German administrator of the Labour Office are allowed to leave the ghetto. Jews who are part of a work brigade, escorted by the police, are also permitted to leave the ghetto area.

4 It is prohibited for Germans and Poles to enter the ghetto. Such entry is permitted only to: the Kreishauptmann or his deputy; a district medical doctor or his deputy; the German police, including the criminal police; an administrator of the Labour Office; Mayors; and those who have passes issued by the Kreishauptmann or one of the departments mentioned under Section 3.

5 A fee of 5 to 500 złoty may be charged for a pass authorizing departure from or entry into the ghetto. The funds shall be divided between the municipality and the Kreishauptmann.

6 On the streets approaching the ghetto, signs must be posted saying [in German and Polish]: *Jüdisches Wohngebiet. Betreten durch Deutsche und Polen verboten.* "Jewish Area: Entry Prohibited to Germans and Poles."

7 Failure to obey these orders is punishable with a fine of up to 1,000 złoty, forced labour, or imprisonment. In cases where a Jewish transgressor cannot pay the fine, the Jewish Council will be held

accountable. Trespassers are liable to arrest. Reporting such violations is mandatory.

8 The permanent closure of access roads and the execution of these orders shall be reported to me no later than February 1941.

9 A copy of this order shall be delivered to the Jewish Council and a receipt obtained.

10 All Mayors and administrators are held responsible for the strict execution of the aforementioned actions pertaining to the free mobility of Jews.

Dr. Rupprecht

Obwieszczenie

Podaję do wiadomości zarządzenie Pana Kreishauptmanna pow. warszawskiego z dnia 10 b. m. dotyczące „żydowskich dzielnic mieszkaniowej i kuracyjnej":

1. Z natychmiastową ważnością zostają żydowskie dzielnice mieszkaniowa i kuracyjna w Otwocku uznane za zamknięte ghetto. Wszystkie drogi dojazdowe, prowadzące do ghetta mają być zamknięte na koszt żydów.

2. Żydom zostaje zabronione opuszczanie ghetta. Do opuszczania ghetta uprawnieni zostają tylko ci żydzi, którzy posiadać będą specjalną przepustkę, wystawioną przez Kreishauptmanna, lub niemieckiego urzędnika Komisarjatu Policji Kryminalnej, bądź przez niemieckiego urzędnika Urzędu Pracy w Otwocku.
Również kolumny robotników mogą [...] ze ghetto, idąc do pracy [...]

3. Niemcom i polakom wstęp do ghetta jest zabroniony bez specjalnych przepustek, które wystawiję niemieckie urzędy, wymienione w P. 2.

4. Wykroczenia będą karane grzywną do 1000 zł lub robotami przymusowymi, albo aresztem. Za wpływ grzywny od żyda odpowiada w razie nieściągalności Rada Żydowska. Wykraczający będą zatrzymywani.

5. Drogą, łączącą żydowską dzielnicę mieszkaniową i kuracyjną, jest wyłącznie ulica Reymonta na odcinku od Samorządowej do Żeromskiego. Po chodniku na tym odcinku żydom chodzić nie wolno.

Burmistrz

JAN GADOMSKI

Otwock, dnia 15 stycznia 1941 r.

U W A G A:

Zabrania się urzędowe obwieszczenia i zarządzenia zrywać, niszczyć, lub uszkadzać, jak również czynić na nich jakiekolwiek dopiski lub uwagi. Wykroczenia przeciwko temu będą surowo karane.

Druk. W. Rzyszczewski, Otwock

ANNOUNCEMENT

In accordance with the decree ordered by the Kreishauptmann, Warsaw district, dated the 10th of this month

Re: The "Jewish Health Resort and Residential Quarters" in Otwock:

1 The Jewish Health Resort and Residential Quarters in Otwock are hereby designated as sealed-off ghettos, effective immediately. All incoming roads leading to the ghetto are to be closed at the expense of the Jews.

2 It is prohibited for all Jews to leave the ghetto. Departure from the ghetto is permissible only to those Jews with permits issued by the Kreishauptmann, a German officer of the criminal police, or a German administrator of the Labour Office in Otwock. Work brigades, escorted by police, may leave the ghetto on their way to work.

3 Germans and Poles are forbidden to enter the ghetto without special passes issued by the German authorities mentioned above, in Section 2.

4 Any infringement of these rules is punishable by a fine of 1,000 złoty, forced labour, or imprisonment. The Jewish Council is responsible for collecting all fines. If fines cannot be collected, the Jewish Council is held accountable. Violators of these rules are subject to arrest.

5 The only road connecting the Jewish Residential Quarters with the Health Resort Quarter is Reymonta Street between Zeromskiego and Samorzadowa Streets. Jews are forbidden to use the sidewalks along this street.

Otwock, January, 15, 1941

MAYOR
Jan Gadomski

Hiermit wird zur öffentlicher Kenntnis gegeben, dass vom heutigen
Tage die Verbindung zwischen dem jüdischen Kurviertel und Wohnviertel
die Samorzadowastrasse von der Reymonta- bis Klonowastrasse ist. Der
Bürgersteig darf auf dieser Strasse nicht von Juden betreten werden.

Der bisherige Verkehr auf der Reymontastrasse ist für Juden nicht
zugelassen.

Otwock, den 8. April 1941.

Ortskommandant   Bürgermeister

Schorr   Jan Gadomski
Hauptmann

OBWIESZCZENIE

Podaje się do publicznej wiadomości, że od dnia dzisiejszego drogą
łączącą żydowskie dzielnice mieszkaniową i kuracyjną jest wyłącznie
ul.Samorzadowa na odcinku od ul.Reymonta do ul.Klonowej. Po chodniku
na tym odcinku żydom chodzić nie wolno.

Dotychczasowa komunikacja ulicą Reymonta dla żydów zostaje skasowa-
na.

Ortskommandant   Burmistrz

Schorr   Jan Gadomski
Hauptmann

Otwock, dnia 8. kwietnia 1941 r.

ANNOUNCEMENT

This is to declare that from this day onwards, the connection between the Jewish Residential Quarter to the Jewish Health Resort Quarter, i.e. the Sanatoria, is Samorzadowa Street, from Reymonta Street to Klonowa Street.

Jews are forbidden to use the sidewalks along this section of the street.

Access to Reymonta Street, permitted to Jews up to this date, is now banned.

Signed

Local Commander
Captain Schorr

Mayor
Jan Gadomski

Otwock, April 30, 1941

KREISHAUPMANN   dnia 28 maja 1941 r.

powiatu warszawskiego   D o

                         Pana Burmistrza

                           w O t w o c k u

Dotyczy: Żydowskiej dzielnicy mieszkaniowej.

      Ponieważ w żydowskiej dzielnicy mieszkaniowej w Otwocku pojawił się tyfus plamisty, zostaje wzbronione opuszczenie tej dzielnicy przez żydów również w dotychczasowych wypadkach wyjątkowych. Wszystkie przepustki bez względu na to przez jaką Władzę zostały wystawione zarówno do opuszczenia dzielnicy żydowskiej jak i do wstępu do niej, tracą aż do odwołania swoją ważność.

      Nowych przepustek na razie wystawiać się nie będzie. Zakaz ten dotyczy również żydów powołanych do pracy.

      Wstęp do ghetta zostaje wszystkim niemcom i polakom z wyjątkiem policji i urzędowego personelu sanitarnego surowo wzbroniony

      Do żydów: którzy będą przebywać poza ghettem będzie się strzelać

      Pozatym w każdym poszczególnym wypadku wykroczeń będą stosowane kary grzywny do 1000 zł. lub aresztu do 6 tygodni.

      Odpis tego zarządzenia należy natychmiast doręczyć Radzie Żydowskiej za pokwitowaniem.

                      /podp./Rupprecht

Za zgodność z oryginałem

Otwock, dnia 28 maja 1941 r.

                K. Chłond
             Sekretarz Miejski

KREISHAUPTMANN
Warsaw District

Otwock, May 28, 1941

To: The Mayor of Otwock

Re: The Jewish Residential Quarters

Due to the break-out of typhoid in the Jewish quarters of Otwock, it is now prohibited for Jews to leave these areas, even in cases of emergency which until now had been sanctioned. All passes for departure and entry to the ghetto, regardless of which authority issued them, are no longer valid.

New passes will not be issued for the foreseeable future. This decree also applies to those Jews who have work assignments.

Entry into the ghetto for all Germans and Poles is strictly prohibited with the exception of the police and government sanitary personnel.

Any Jew found outside the ghetto will be shot.

Furthermore, a fee of up to 1,000 złoty or a detention of up to six weeks will be administered for any violation of this decree.

A copy of this decree shall be delivered immediately to the Jewish Council and a receipt obtained.

Sub. Lieutenant/ Rupprecht

Otwock, May 28, 1941

K. Chlond,
Town Secretary

Obwieszczenie

Dotyczy: kary śmierci za nieuprawnione opuszczenie żydowskich dzielnic mieszkaniowych.

W ostatnim czasie rozprzestrzenili żydzi, którzy opuścili wyznaczone im dzielnice mieszkaniowe, w licznych udowodnionych wypadkach tyfus plamisty. Aby zapobiec grożącemu w ten sposób niebezpieczeństwu dla ludności, rozporządził Generalny Gubernator, że żyd, który w przyszłości opuści nieuprawniony wyznaczoną mu dzielnicę mieszkaniową, będzie karany śmiercią.

Tej samej karze podlega ten, kto takim żydom udziela świadomie schronienia lub im w inny sposób pomaga (np. przez udostępnienie noclegu, utrzymania, przez zabranie na pojazdy wszelkiego rodzaju itp.).

Osądzenie nastąpi przez Sąd Specjalny w Warszawie.

Zwracam całej ludności Okręgu Warszawskiego wyraźnie uwagę na to nowe postanowienie ustawowe, ponieważ odtąd będzie stosowana bezlitosna surowość.

Warszawa, dnia 10 listopada 1941.

(–) Dr FISCHER
Gubernator

PUBLIC ANNOUNCEMENT

DEATH PENALTY FOR THOSE LEAVING THE DESIGNATED JEWISH QUARTER

Recently it has been confirmed that Jews in the designated Jewish Residential Quarters have spread the typhus virus.

In order to prevent this threat from reaching the general population, the Governor-General has determined that any Jew who leaves the designated areas will be punished by death.

Persons who knowingly provide Jews with shelter or any other type of assistance (nightly accommodation, transportation of any kind) will be subject to the same punishment.

Sentencing will take place in Warsaw at a special court sitting.

The general public in the Warsaw district should be aware of the seriousness of this decree.

Henceforth, non-compliance with this ruling will be prosecuted without mercy.

Warsaw, November 10, 1941

Dr. Fischer
GOVERNOR

Warszawa, dnia 25. grudnia 1941 r.

Komisarz

Dzielnicy Żydowskiej w Warszawie

Adg. Nr. 7/41

ZARZĄDZENIE

Dotyczy: WYDANIA PRZEDMIOTÓW FUTRZANYCH

Wszystkie znajdujące się w posiadaniu Żydów płaszcze futrzane, okrycia futrzane, kołnierze futrzane, jak również wszystkie inne futra i skóry futrzane bez względu na rodzaj i niezależnie od tego czy obrobione czy też nieobrobione, winny być do dnia 28 grudnia 1941 r. włącznie oddane.

Przedmioty powyższe mają być dostarczone w następujących miejscach:

a. przy ulicy Grzybowskiej 26/28 (gmach główny Rady Żydowskiej)

b. przy ulicy Grzybowskiej 27 (Wydział Zabezpieczonych Nieruchomości przy Radzie Żydowskiej)

Żydzi, u których po upływie terminu dostarczenia będą znalezione przedmioty podlegające obowiązkowi oddania, zostaną rozstrzelani.

Zarządzenie niniejsze wchodzi w życie z dniem 25.XII.1941 r.

(—) A U E R S W A L D

"Monolit", Warszawa, Chłodna 8.

ZGODNE Z ORYGINAŁEM

WARSAW, DECEMBER 25, 1941

COMMISSIONER
Jewish District of Warsaw

DECREE REGARDING: DELIVERY OF FUR ARTICLES

All fur coats, fur coverings, fur collars and all other fur articles which are in the possession of Jews, regardless of type and condition, are to be turned in by December 28, 1941.

The articles above are to be delivered to the following places:
a. 26/28 Grzybowska Street (the main building of the Jewish Council)
b. 27 Grzybowska Street (Department of Insured Property, Jewish Council)

Jews who are found to be in possession of the above articles after final delivery date will be shot.

This announcement is valid as of December 25, 1941.

AUERSWALD

BEKANNTMACHUNG

Betrifft:
Beherbergung von geflüchteten Juden.

Es besteht Anlass zu folgendem Hinweis:
Gemäss der 3. Verordnung über Aufenthalts-
beschränkungen im Generalgouvernement
vom 15.10.1941 (VO. Bl. GG. S. 595) unterliegen
Juden, die den jüdischen Wohnbezirk unbe-
fugt verlassen, der Todesstrafe.

Gemäss der gleichen Vorschrift unterliegen Perso-
nen, die solchen Juden wissentlich Unterschlupf gewähren, Beköstigung verabfolgen oder Nahrungsmittel verkaufen, ebenfalls der Todesstrafe.

Die nichtjüdische Bevölkerung wird da-
her dringend gewarnt:

1.) Juden Unterschlupf zu gewähren,

2.) Juden Beköstigung zu verabfolgen,

3.) Juden Nahrungsmittel zu verkaufen.

Tschenstochau, den 24. 9. 42.

OGŁOSZENIE

Dotyczy:
przetrzymywania ukrywających się żydów.

Zachodzi potrzeba przypomnienia, że stosownie do § 3 Rozporządzenia o ograniczeniach
pobytu w Gen. Gub. z dnia 15. X. 1941 roku
(Dz. Rozp. dla GG. str. 595) żydzi, opuszczający
dzielnicę żydowską bez zezwolenia, podlegają
karze śmierci.

Według tego rozporządzenia, osobom, które takim
żydom świadomie udzielają przytułku, dostarczają im
jedzenia lub sprzedają artykuły żywnościowe, grozi
również kara śmierci.

Niniejszym ostrzega się stanowczo ludność
nieżydowską przed:

1.) udzielaniem żydom przytułku,

2.) dostarczaniem im jedzenia,

3.) sprzedawaniem im artykułów
żywnościowych.

Częstochowa, dnia 24. 9. 42.

Der Stadthauptmann
Dr. Franke

ANNOUNCEMENT REGARDING:
THE SHELTERING OF FUGITIVE JEWS

The circumstances make the following notice necessary:
In accordance with the third decree on the limitations of stay inside the Generalgouvernement dated from October 15, 1941 (VO. Bl. GG. Page 595), Jews who leave the Jewish Quarter without permission are subject to the death penalty.

According to the same decree, individuals who knowingly provide shelter, food or sell provisions to such Jews are also subject to the death penalty.

THIS IS A STRONG WARNING
TO THE NON-JEWISH POPULATION AGAINST:

1 Providing shelter to Jews
2 Providing Jews with food
3 Selling provisions to Jews

Tschenstochau, September 24, 1942

CITY GOVERNOR [*DER STADTHAUPTMANN*]
Dr. Franke

Photographs

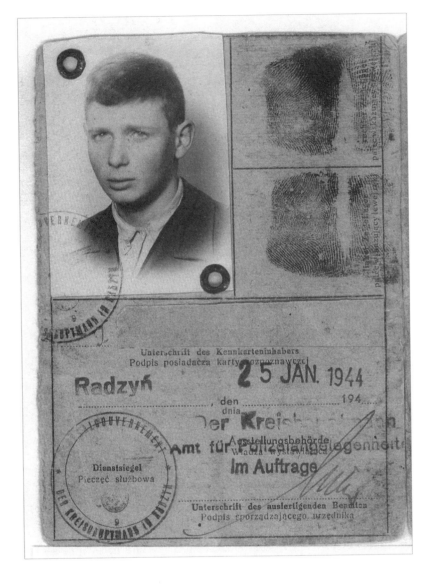

Unterschrift des Kennkarteninhabers
Podpis posiadacza karty rozpoznawczej

Radzyń
..................................., den ....194...
dnia

Der Kreis..............................
Ausstellungsbehörde
Amt für...
Im Auftrage

2 5 JAN. 1944

Dienstsiegel
Pieczęć służbowa

Unterschrift des ausfertigenden Beamten
Podpis sporządzającego urzędnika

(Both pages) The *Kennkarte* – identity card required by the German regulations during World War II – that Marian Domanski acquired to "prove" that he was not Jewish.

1   Marian's school, School No. 2, viewed from Karczewska Street. The photo was
    taken in 2005. (Photo courtesy of Piotr Cmiel)

2   The Świder River, which flows near Otwock. (Photo courtesy of Jan Tabencki)

The Villa Maria on Samorzadowa Street, Otwock. During the German occupation, it housed the headquarters of the Jewish ghetto police. (Photo courtesy of Justyna Gornowicz)

One of the gates in the Otwock ghetto, on Warszawska Street, guarded by a German soldier. (Photo courtesy of Otwock Museum)

1

2

1 A house with thatched roof typical of those in the region where Marian Domanski spent the war. It is similar to the house outside Włodawa where he was offered
lodging while he was on his way to see his family in Dubeczno in April 1942. The
photo was taken by the author in 1993.

2 Paul Siedlecki's farm near Łuków, where Marian stayed in the summer of 1943.
The photo was taken by the author in 1993.

1

2

1 The deportation of Otwock Jews to Treblinka on August 19, 1942. The photo was taken by a passenger from a passing train. (Photo courtesy of Jewish Historical Institute, Warsaw)

2 The memorial commemorating the mass murder of 2,000 Otwock Jews after the liquidation of the Otwock ghetto.

Marian Domanski at about seventeen years old. The photo was taken while he was working in a photo studio in Dzierżoniów in 1946.

Marian at the swimming pool in Piotrolesie in 1947.

Marian at the air force technical school in Bemowo, 1950.

Krystyna Danko from Otwock, who hid and provided for the Kokoszko family.
She was awarded the title of Righteous Among the Nations from the Yad Vashem
Martyrs' and Heroes' Remembrance Authority in 1999. Warsaw, 2007.

The Karczew cemetery in Otwock, where most of the gravestones have been overturned or built over. At the time of the war, the cemetery was on the outskirts of Otwock. This photo was taken by the author in 1993.

Index

The Azrieli Foundation was established in 1989 to realize and extend the philanthropic vision of David J. Azrieli, C.M., C.Q., M.Arch. The Foundation's mission is to support a wide spectrum of initiatives in education and research. The Azrieli Foundation is an active supporter of programs in the fields of Jewish education, the education of architects, scientific and medical research, and education in the arts. The Azrieli Foundation's many well-known initiatives include: the Holocaust Survivor Memoirs Program, which collects, preserves, publishes and distributes the written memoirs of survivors in Canada; the Azrieli Institute for Educational Empowerment, an innovative program successfully working to keep at-risk youth in school; and the Azrieli Fellows Program, which promotes academic excellence and leadership on the graduate level at Israeli universities.